Parallel Computational Geometry

A Aggarwal[1], B Chazelle[2], L Guibas[3,4], C Ó'Dúnlaing[5,6,], C Yap[5,*]*

1 IBM Thomas J Watson Research Center
Yorktown Heights, New York 10598

2 Department of Computer Science
Princeton University
Princeton, New Jersey 08544

3 Digital Equipment Corporation Systems Research Laboratories
130 Lytton Avenue
Palo Alto, California 94301

4 Computer Science Department
Stanford University
Stanford, California 94305

5 Courant Institute of Mathematical Sciences
New York University
251 Mercer Street
New York, New York 10012

6 School of Mathematics
Trinity College
Dublin 2
Irish Republic

ABSTRACT

We present efficient parallel algorithms for several basic problems in computational geometry convex hulls, Voronoi diagrams, detecting line segment intersections, triangulating simple polygons, minimizing a circumscribing triangle, and recursive datastructures for 3-dimensional queries

July 14, 1987

* The work of these authors is supported by NSF grants #DCR 84-01898 and #DCR-84-01633

1. Introduction

Computational geometry addresses algorithmic problems in diverse areas such as VLSI design, robotics, and computer graphics Since 1975 there has been a wide development of sequential algorithms for geometric problems, but until 1985 there was little published about developing parallel algorithms for such problems A notable exception was the Ph D research of Anita Chow (1980) which seems to have been the pioneering work in the field but unfortunately only a portion of it has appeared in the open literature

This paper contributes some parallel algorithms for solving geometric problems

(1) Convex hulls in two and three dimensions

(2) Voronoi diagrams and proximity problems

(3) Detecting segment intersections and triangulating a polygon

(4) Polygon optimization problems

(5) Creating data structures in two and three dimensions to answer some standard queries

It is seldom obvious how to generate parallel algorithms in this area since popular techniques such as contour tracing, plane sweeping, or gift wrapping involve an explicitly sequential (iterative) approach (see [Preparata and Shamos (1985)] for more details) In this paper we exploit data-structures that are simple enough to compute efficiently in parallel while being powerful enough to answer queries efficiently However, the queries may be answered slightly less efficiently than would be possible if the data-structures were constructed sequentially 'Efficient' here means polylogarithmic in parallel time

All the algorithms presented here will be NC-algorithms, i e , algorithms executable in polylog depth on polynomial-size circuits We caution that the circuits here are slightly different from those used in machine-based complexity theory in that each node of our circuit can compute an infinite precision arithmetic operation Furthermore these algorithms shall all be described as if they were implemented on a *CREW PRAM* -- a concurrent-read, exclusive-write parallel random access machine Such a machine is conceived as having a large number of processors with common access to a common memory Any number of processors can read the same memory cell simultaneously in $O(1)$ steps, and any processor can write to a memory cell in $O(1)$ steps, but if two processors attempt to write to the same cell simultaneously then the machine enters an undefined state

We should mention here that Anita Chow's dissertation pays close attention to the model of computation involved, and in several cases she provides algorithms for implementation on two models of parallel computation the CREW PRAM model, and the cube-connected cycles (CCC) network. As mentioned before, in the CREW model, all the processors share the same memory, however, in the CCC network, each processor has its own memory, and is connected to at most four other processors For details on the CCC model, see [Chow (1980)]

It follows from [Kozen and Yap (1985)] that most common computational geometry problems including all the problems considered in this paper have, in principle, NC-algorithms Recall that they combined the techniques of [Ben-Or, Kozen and Reif (1984)] and [Collins (1975)] to give parallel algorithms for computing cell decompositions with adjacency information, for fixed dimensions, these algorithms are in NC The consequences of the cell decomposition algorithm for parallel computational geometry are explored more carefully in [Yap (1987)] Since any appeal to [Kozen and Yap (1985)] involves a reduction to Tarski's language for real closed fields, and the methods are too general to be of much practical use, this furnishes an existence proof for NC algorithms rather than furnishing practical NC algorithms

Many of the problems considered here are known to have $\Omega(n \log (n))$ lower bounds in the algebraic computation tree model [Ben-Or (1983)] Therefore the goal in our research in such cases is to aim for $\Omega(\log (n))$ parallel time when $O(n)$ processors are available Only in some instances do we present such optimal algorithms, and the algorithms may require a preprocessing step which involves sorting While $O(\log^2(n))$ sorting networks have been known for many years, to ensure optimality we may need to invoke an optimal parallel sorting method ($\log (n)$ parallel time) The AKS sorting network achieves these bounds but with utterly unacceptable overhead (at the present state of knowledge see [Ajtai, Komlós and Szemerédi (1983), Leighton (1984), Cole and Ó'Dúnlaing (1986)]) More recently an optimal PRAM algorithm has been described which has much lower overhead [Cole (1986)] In our algorithms to compute the Voronoi diagram for a planar point set and convex hull in three dimensions, we are able to avoid sorting even though we only match the complexity bounds of Anita Chow

Also we shall pay some attention to the processor allocation problem a *PRAM* algorithm cannot be considered completely described until one has a clear description of how the various tasks are to be allocated among the available pool of processors Such considerations usually become unimportant when the time taken to complete a parallel step is logarithmic (or worse) in the number of processors involved, since processor allocation is usually easy to accomplish in logarithmic parallel time

Two standard methods of parallel algorithm design will be exploited freely throughout this paper computing a running sum ('parallel prefix'), and list-ranking To compute a running sum means to compute the n initial sums of an array of n numbers This is easily computed in logarithmic parallel time with n processors, by imagining a balanced binary tree whose leaves are the array entries at each internal node the sum of the entries of all its leaf descendants can be computed (in an upward parallel sweep), and from these internal sums all initial sums can be computed in a second phase List-ranking involves traversing a linked list and determining the rank (distance from the end) of all its entries This can be accomplished in logarithmic parallel time by a pointer-jumping technique, it is discussed briefly at the end of Section 3

2. Definitions and terms.

As stated in the Introduction, the algorithms treated here will all belong to the class NC, but we shall express them as *PRAM* algorithms running on a *CREW* machine The notation

$$NC_k^+(f(n))$$

will indicate the class of algorithms running on a *PRAM* using $f(n)$ processors and halting in $O(\log^k(n))$ steps We are mainly interested in the class $NC_k^+(n)$, i e those using a linear number of processors Note We use 'NC^+' instead of 'NC' to distinguish our model from the circuit model of machine-based complexity See [Yap (1987)]

We let E^2 (respectively, E^3) denote the Euclidean plane (respectively, Euclidean 3-space) In this paper, we restrict our attention to E^2 or E^3 Given a (finite and nonempty) set S of points in E^2 or E^3, the *convex hull* $H(S)$ is the smallest convex set containing all points in S Sometimes by abuse of notation we shall confuse the convex hull with the polygon (respectively, polyhedron) which constitutes its boundary We use the notation $\partial H(S)$ to denote the polygonal boundary of $H(S)$

Given a finite nonempty set S of points in E^2, its *Voronoi diagram* $Vor(S)$ is defined as follows For each point p in S, define the *Voronoi cell* $V(p)$ as the set of points z in E^2 such that z is as close to p as to any other point in S Recall that the Voronoi cells are all nonempty closed convex sets with polygonal boundaries and two cells can meet only along their common boundaries (i e , the interior of every cell is disjoint from all other cells) The *Voronoi diagram* $Vor(S)$ is defined as the planar point-set formed from the union of the boundaries of all the Voronoi cells, it is a planar graph with $O(n)$ edges and vertices, all the edges are straight line-segments (perhaps unbounded), and two cells can have at most one edge in common

3 Optimal Parallel Convex Hull in the Plane

Fast parallel algorithms for the planar convex hull problem have been considered in the recent literature [Nath et al (1981), Chow (1981), Akl (1983), Chazelle (1984)] The algorithms typically use a simple divide-and-conquer technique, recursively computing the convex hull of n points by solving two problems of half the size It seems that any such technique requires $\Omega(\log^2(n))$ time The main result in this section is the following

Theorem 1 *The problem of computing the convex hull of a set of points in the plane is in $NC_1^*(n)$*

We subsequently learned that Atallah and Goodrich (1985), and Wagener (1985, 1987), have independently used a similar technique to derive the same result

From the well-known fact that sorting can be reduced to the planar convex hull problem, or using the lower bounds for the algebraic computation tree model in [Ben-Or (1983)], it follows that the $\log(n)$ time is optimal for n processors Actually the algorithm is optimal in a stronger sense it follows from the work of Cook and Dwork (1982) that $O(\log(n))$ time is the best possible *even* if we allow arbitrarily many processors

Let S be the given set of n points Use the pair of points on the convex hull $H(S)$ with maximum and minimum x-coordinate to partition $H(S)$ into two parts in the natural way the *upper* and the *lower* chains By symmetry, it is sufficient to show how to compute the upper chain in $O(\log(n))$ time First sort S according to the x-coordinate of the points, using $O(\log(n))$ time with n processors [Ajtai, Komlós and Szemerédi (1983), Leighton (1984), Cole (1986)] At this stage, covertical sets of points can be detected and all but the highest from each set discarded in $O(\log(n))$ steps Our algorithm divides S into $\sqrt{n}$ sets of $\sqrt{n}$ points, recursively computes the upper convex chain of each set, and then merges all these chains together in $O(\log(n))$ time The details of merging are non-trivial

Let us see how to merge $\sqrt{n}$ upper chains in $O(\log(n))$ steps with n processors First consider two upper chains C and C' Since we divide S by x-coordinate, this ensures that the x-coordinates of any 2 chains do not overlap Granted that their edges are presented in an array in sorted order, a single processor can compute in $O(\log(n))$ time the unique line which is tangent to both chains, together with the two points of tangency. This was shown by Overmars and Van Leeuwen (1981) Since there are at most $\left\lceil \dfrac{\sqrt{n}}{2} \right\rceil$

common tangents to be computed n processors can compute all such tangents in time $O(\log(n))$ Note that processor allocation raises no difficulty here since all the chains have a natural sequence (according to their x-coordinates) and there is a natural sequence therefore on the set of all pairs of chains

Let G denote the (combinatorial) graph whose vertices are the points in S and whose edges are the edges in the upper chains, together with the line-segments defined by the tangent lines just discussed. There are at most $n-1$ edges in all the upper chains, and they can be compressed into contiguous locations in an array A by using a running-sum technique (in $O(\log(n))$ parallel time) The extra $\left\lceil \frac{\sqrt{n}}{2} \right\rceil < n$ edges may be appended to these edges in the upper chains The array A contains two directed edges (x_1,x_2) and (x_2,x_1) for each undirected edge $\{x_1,x_2\}$ Using an optimal parallel sorting method, sort these edges according to

(slope of edge) within (earlier x-coordinate)

The slope of an edge is the angle it makes with the x-axis, measured from $-\pi/2$ to $3\pi/2$ (with $\pi/2$ corresponding to the vertical upwards direction) Thus the array is partitioned into adjacency lists for the vertices of G

From G we can identify vertices of the upper chain of S using the following observation Consider any point v in S, which is neither leftmost nor rightmost in S If v belongs to the upper chain of S, let u and w be the vertices immediately before and after v along the chain Clearly the slopes of the edges (v,u) and (v,w) are adjacent among all the edges out of v, and the angle uvw (measured clockwise from u to w) is $\geq \pi$ Clearly, for each vertex v there can be at most one pair of edges (v,u) and (v,w) with this property, and such vertices v can be detected in constant time with one processor per edge in the array A. Thus criterion identifies all edges and vertices on the upper chain, and perhaps some others, except for the first and last edges on the upper chain these are, of course, the edges with maximum and minimum slopes respectively leaving the leftmost and rightmost vertices (Since S is presorted by x-coordinate it is easy to identify these two vertices)

For all these triples u,v,w which indicate possible vertices of the upper chain, let us call v a 'candidate' and w its 'successor' If v is not a candidate its successor is undefined, and the leftmost vertex has as its successor the next vertex on the upper chain As indicated above this is easily identified. This successor relation defines a forest of trees, in which the upper chain is represented by a branch connecting the leftmost vertex to the rightmost This branch can be identified in logarithmic parallel time, one processor per vertex, using the parallel ranking technique described below

To complete our inductive step, we now must collect the vertices of the upper chain of S into consecutive locations in an array This is easily accomplished using parallel prefix, i e , computing a running sum on an array $C(v)$ whose entry is 1 if v is in the upper chain and 0 otherwise This completes the merge process of our algorithm

Since the ranking problem is so basic and will be used again it bears repeating here Here we consider the successor relation as defining a forest of trees directed from child to parent, and the rank of a node in this forest is its distance from its root ancestor In view of a later application, in addition to the rank information, we compute an additional $O(\log(n))$ pointers for each vertex

(*) In $\log(n)$ parallel time, each node can learn its rank and also for each $i \le \log(n)$, it also holds a pointer to its 2^i-th successor, if it has such a successor

This is done in two phases, each phase taking $\log(n)$ parallel time. In the first phase, by the well-known doubling technique, every vertex determines for all $i \le \log(n)$ whether it has a 2^i-th successor, and if so, which. In the second phase, at stage i (there are $\log(n)$ stages) all vertices with rank between 2^i and $2^{i+1}-1$ learn their exact rank. It is easy to implement all this on a *CREW PRAM* in logarithmic time

The runtime $T(n)$ of this convex hull algorithm, for n points with n processors, satisfies the relation

$$T(n) \le c \log(n) + T(\sqrt{n})$$

which implies $T(n)$ is $O(\log(n))$

4. Voronoi Diagram and Proximity Problems

One of the fundamental data structures of computational geometry is the Voronoi diagram [Shamos (1977)] The first optimal sequential algorithm to compute the Voronoi diagram was given by Shamos and Hoey (1975) and it takes $O(n \log n)$ time. In this section, we show

Theorem 2. *There is an $NC_2^*(n)$ algorithm for the planar Voronoi diagram of a set of points Furthermore, the algorithm only assumes an $NC_2^*(n)$ sorting algorithm*

Shamos (1977) also pointed out that the Voronoi diagram can be used as a powerful tool to give efficient algorithms for a wide variety of other geometric proximity problems From the Voronoi diagram we can easily obtain the closest pair of sites (points), or the closest neighbor of each site, or the Euclidean minimum spanning tree of the n sites, or the largest point-free circle with center inside their convex hull, etcetera. Efficient reductions for these problems are possible in our parallel computation model, so our polylog result for the Voronoi also implies polylog algorithms for all these problems, using a linear number of processors Note that there is a well-known reduction of the Voronoi diagram of a set of points in the plane to the convex hull of a set of points in 3-space [Brown (1979), Guibas and Stolfi (1983)]. Also, in her thesis, Anita Chow (1980) shows that the three-dimensional convex hull can be computed in $NC_3^*(n)$, and exploits this to give an $O(\log^3(n))$ algorithm to compute the diagram However, her methods frequently involve optimal time parallel sorting[1], which the following direct method avoids In our FOCS extended abstract we gave an $NC_3^*(n)$ algorithm which avoids optimal time parallel sort. In the present paper, we improve this to $NC_2^*(n)$ by exploiting a simple observation suggested by Goodrich.

The present algorithm for computing the Voronoi diagram is modelled after the sequential method first presented by Shamos and Hoey [1975] This is a divide-and-conquer method in which two Voronoi diagrams for the respective sets P and Q of points (where these sets are *vertically separated*, i e , there is a vertical line L which has all of P to its left and all of Q to its right) are merged in linear time to a diagram for $P \cup Q$ The merging is defined by a polygonal path (the 'contour' or 'seam') separating P from Q, the process is akin to tracing a line and seems inherently sequential The contour separates the plane into the set of points closer to P than to Q (i e , the set of points x whose closest point or points in S are all in P) and

---

[1] The runtime bound given in [Chow (1980)] differs from the bound quoted here by an additional factor of $\log \log(n)$ These discrepancies arise wherever sorting is involved The $O(\log(n) \log \log(n))$ parallel sorting algorithm in [Valiant (1975)] has since been superseded by theoretically optimal algorithms

those closer to Q than to P

The following illustrates the contour between two hypothetical sets P and Q

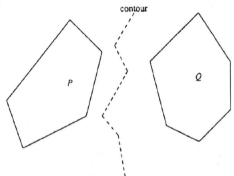

Figure 1 Merging by contour-tracing

Our goal is to parallelize this contour tracing. Let us introduce some suitable terminology The convex hull $H(S)$ has already been defined The *normals* of S are defined as the half-lines extending from the corners of $H(S)$ and perpendicular to the sides incident to those corners two normals extend from each corner These normals partition the complement of $H(S)$, $E^2 - H(S)$, into *sectors*, which are alternately *slices* (V-shaped) and *strips* (bounded by a side of $H(S)$ and the two incident normals). The following picture clarifies this terminology

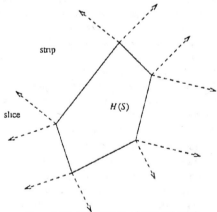

Figure 2 Normals and sectors (slices and strips)

The points of intersection of $Vor(S)$ with the convex polygon $\partial H(S)$ we call the *cutpoints* (figure 3) Let U be the strip defined by an edge e of the convex hull The set $U \cap Vor(S)$ we call the *e-promontory* We will assume that S is in general position (no three points collinear, no four concyclic) Together with the convexity of the Voronoi cells, this implies that the promontory has the natural structure of a binary tree with leaves at the cutpoints and such that the parent of a node is always more distant from e Beyond the root of this binary tree extends an infinite ray that bisects the strip

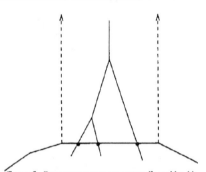

Figure 3 Promontory: cutpoints are indicated by (•)

Point location inside strips is easily done in $O(\log^2(n))$ serial time We now modify a suggestion of Goodrich to show that $O(\log(n))$ serial time suffices.

Lemma 3. *Suppose a strip has an e-promontory with k vertices and edges There is a k processor $O(\log(k))$ time parallel algorithm for constructing a data-structure for the plane partition defined by the e-promontory so that in $O(\log(k))$ time a single processor can answer a point location query*

Proof The e-promontory is a complete binary tree laid out in the plane. We may assume that each leaf is on the x-axis, and for every node v all its descendants have smaller y-coordinate. For any node v of the promontory, let T_v denote the subtree of the e-promontory rooted at v Each internal node v of the e-promontory tree may be associated with a triangular region R_v with v as one corner of the triangle and the two other corners the extreme cutpoints below the subtree at v By convexity of Voronoi cells, the entire subtree T_v is contained in R_v Suppose p is a query point inside the strip Let r be the root of the e-promontory. The interesting case is when p lies inside R_r, and this can be checked in constant time We can now do a binary search inside R_r by locating a vertex v such that T_v contains between 1/3 and 2/3 of the vertices of T_r If p is inside T_v, we can recursively do point location for p inside this subtree Otherwise, let we next search inside a modified version of T_r the modified tree T'_r consists of replacing T_v by three vertices corresponding to the corners of the triangle R_v, together with the two edges from v to the other two corners This recursive search can be carried out in $O(\log(k))$ serial time

It remains to construct a search structure D_r for the tree T_r. The search structure D_r consists of a binary tree whose internal nodes are associated with triangular regions of the form R_v which we use for comparisons if we are at some internal node z of D_r, we next go to the right (resp. left) child of z if query point p lies inside (resp. outside) the triangular region of z To construct D_r associated with T_r, we do an important preprocessing step where for each node v we determine its preorder rank $rank(v)$ in the tree and from this, we easily deduce $maxrank(v)$, the maximum rank of its descendants This can be done using k processors and $O(\log(k))$ time [Tarjan and Vishkin (1985)].[2] We will deduce two important pieces of

---

[2] Their CRCW parallel RAM algorithm can be adapted for our CREW version

information from these computed values First, the number $desc(v)$ of descendants of a node v is given by $1+maxrank(v)-rank(v)$ Second, we can decide in constant time if any given vertex u is a descendant of another v More precisely, u is a descendant of v iff

$$rank(v) \leq rank(u) \leq maxrank(v)$$

Inductively, suppose we have to construct a search structure D_r for the subtree T_r rooted at some node r We assume that $aesc(v)$ is precomputed for each v in T_r In particular, let $k = desc(r)$ be the number of nodes in T_r Assigning one processor to each vertex of T_r, in $O(1)$ steps, we can locate the deepest node of T_r with at least $2k/3$ descendants, and choose the node v_0 to be that one of its children with the larger number of descendants (breaking ties arbitrarily) It is easy to see that v_0 will have between $k/3$ and $2k/3$ descendants The root of D_r will be associated with the region R_r The right subtree of (the root of) D_r will be recursively constructed from T_{v_0} note that the precomputed information $desc(v)$ for each node of T_{v_0} is available with no further work Let T'_r be the modified tree obtained by pruning T_{v_0} as described above We want to recursively construct the left subtree of D_r from T'_r But first we must revise the precomputed information $desc(v)$ for each node for T'_r To do this, we only need to update the value of $desc(v)$ by subtracting $desc(v_0)-2$ from $desc(v)$ for all v that are ancestors of v_0 But this is easy since with one processor per vertex, each vertex can in constant time deduce if it is an ancestor of v_0 (use the preorder numbering of nodes as shown above) Note that to represent the partition of the nodes of T_r into two sets (belonging to T_{v_0} and to T'_r respectively), it is enough to have each node of T_r keep a pointer to one of the children of the root r in D_r The region R_r can be written into a location associated with r Q.E D

The above data-structure will help us to form the contour efficiently Let us introduce some simple notation Recall that a recursive step in the algorithm will involve separating a given set S by a vertical line L into two sets $P \cup Q$ (where P is to the left of L and Q to its right), recursively constructing $Vor(P)$ and $Vor(Q)$ separately and merging the two along the contour We shall speak of the edges of $Vor(P)$ and $Vor(Q)$ as PP-edges and QQ-edges In the combined Voronoi diagram the contour edges can be called PQ edges in an obvious extension of this notation, and the vertices can be classified as PPP, PPQ, PQQ, and QQQ, depending on whether the associated three points of S (assuming general position so no four are cocyclic) involve 3, 2, 1, or no points of P.

We need therefore to identify the PPQ and PQQ vertices Instead of computing them directly, we solve the following simpler problem to identify the PP and QQ edges that intersect the contour We postpone till later determining precisely where they meet the contour

To carry this out, we need one more preliminary computation This is necessitated by the fact that a Voronoi edge may intersect the contour twice [3] However we can break up each Voronoi edge into at most two 'semi-edges' such that the contour meets each semi-edge at most once let e be any edge of $Vor(P)$ determined by the two points u, v in P If the horizontal ray emanating leftward from u or v intersects e at some point x (this happens with at most one of the rays from u and v) then we split e into two semi-edges at x If neither ray intersects e then the entire edge e constitutes a semi-edge Similarly, if e is an edge of $Vor(Q)$, we would split e into at most two semi-edges using the horizontal rays emanating rightward from

---

[3] We are indebted to Hubert Wagener (private communication) for pointing this out to us

u or *v*

Lemma 4. *Each semi-edge intersects the contour at most once*

Proof (sketch). Let *e* be an edge separating points *u* and *v* of *P* in *Vor*(*P*) Since any intersection of the contour with *e* results in a *PPQ* vertex, which will be an endpoint of an edge, call it *e′*, separating *u* and *v* in the combined diagram, we conclude that the contour cannot intersect *e* more than twice Suppose that it intersects *e* twice Then *e′* together with the contour would enclose one of these points, *u* say, completely, and since the contour is monotonic in the *y*-direction it is easy to see that the horizontal line extending left-wards from *u* intersects the edge *e′* Thus each intersection point is on a different semi-edge of *e*. Q.E D

Call any semi-edge that intersects the contour *relevant*. Note that an semi-edge in *Vor*(*P*) is relevant if and only if one endpoint is closer to *P* and the other endpoint is closer to *Q* To decide if a Voronoi vertex (or other point bounding a semi-edge) *v* of *Vor*(*P*) is closer to *P* than to *Q*, we have two cases (i) If *v* is left of *L* then we determine the slice or strip of *H*(*Q*) containing *v* If *v* is in a slice, then *v* is closest to a unique point *q* in *Q*, we can decide easily if *v* is closer to *q* than to the closest points of *P* If *v* is in a strip, we reduce the problem to point location inside a strip, once we have located *v* in the appropriate cell of *Vor*(*Q*) we can compare distances as in the case of the slice. (ii) If *v* is right of *L* it may initially appear that we need a general point location data-structure for that part of *Vor*(*Q*) lying to the right of *L* We show how to avoid this using another idea

We need some new terminology Consider the set of points *x* to the right of *L* such that the circle centered at *x* and tangential to *L* passes through some point *q* ∈ *Q* but where the interior of the circle contains no other points of *Q*. The set of such points will be call the *beachline* (of *Q*) (Alternatively, we could have defined the beach to be the 'contour' separating *L* from *Q*) For any point *q* not in *L*, let the *q*-*parabola* be the parabola focused at *q* with directrix *L*. (See figure 4).

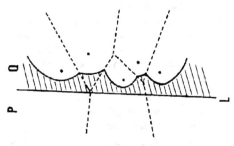

Figure 4 The beachline (the beachhead *B* is shaded)

Lemma 5.

(a)   The beachline is a simple curve, disjoint from *L* and projecting monotonically onto *L* Thus the beachline divides the half-plane to the right of *L* into two connected regions The region that is adjacent to *L* is called the *beachhead* and denoted by *B* The beachhead is characterized as the set of those points in the right half-plane of *L* that are closer to *L* than to any point in *Q*

(b)   The beachline is composed of a finite sequence of parabolic arcs, each such parabola being a portion of some q-parabola, $q \in Q$ Each such q is said to be *near L* The point where two parabolic arcs meet is called a *transition point*

(c)   *Let C be the contour defined by the partition $S = P \cup Q$ Then C lies entirely to the left of the beachline*

(d)   *The Voronoi cells of $Vor(Q)$ that intersect B are precisely those belonging to points q that are near L in the sense of (b) Each connected component in the restriction of $Vor(Q)$ to B has the structure of a free tree embedded in the plane whose leaves are on the boundary of B at most one leaf is on L The intersection of a cell of $Vor(Q)$ with the beachhead may have several connected components Each such component is called a B-cell The B-cells are linearly ordered along the beachline*

(e)   *Let x be a transition point Then there are two points $q, q' \in Q$ such that x lies on an edge of $Vor(Q)$ separating the cells of q and q' Moreover the two parabolic arcs that meet at x are portions of the q- and q'-parabolas, respectively*

Proof (a) To see that the beachline projects monotonically onto e, for each point p on L, draw the horizontal ray R emanating rightward from p The beach line intersects R at a unique point x such that the points on R closer to L than to Q are precisely those lying between p and x

(b) The points x of the beachline where the circle centered at x and tangent to L is incident to two or more points of Q are finitely many in number These define the transition points For non-transition points x on the beachline, the circle at x touches a unique $q \in Q$ Such an x lies on the parabola focused at q Thus the beachline is composed of a finite number of parabolic arcs that are joined together at transition points

(c) Let x be a point on the contour, and let D be the largest disc centered at x whose interior does not contain any point of $P \cup Q$ Then D touches points both in P and Q since x is on the contour; therefore its interior intersects L Were x to the right of the beachline it would follow that D contained points of Q in its interior, a contradiction, hence x is on or to the left of the beachline.

(d) Clearly a point in Q is near L if and only if its cell in $Vor(Q)$ intersects B Since every point in Q is obviously to the right of the beachline, every B-cell must intersect the beachline and therefore the B-cells are linearly ordered by their intersections with the beachline For the same reason each connected component of $B \cap Vor(Q)$ is acyclic and has the structure of a (free) tree whose leaves are on the boundary of B If such a component met the line L twice then there would be a chain of edges connecting these two points within B and therefore there would exist some B-cells not meeting the beachline hence at most one leaf is on L.

(e) Choose q and q' to be the points that define the parabolic arcs that meet at x Q.E D

Lemma 6. *In $O(\log(n))$ time with $O(n)$ processors, we can construct the beachline of Q and a suitable data-structure to do the following query For any point v, to determine in $O(\log(n))$ serial time, whether v lies in the beachhead B and, if so, which B-cell contains v*

Proof Using one processor per edge of $Vor(Q)$, we can compute all the transition points (at most 2) on that edge To see this, let e be an edge separating the Voronoi cells of q and q' in $Vor(Q)$ Then at each point x (at most 2) where the q-parabola intersects e, we get x is a transition point Once all the transition points are computed, we may sort them by their y-coordinates (using list-ranking) to form the beachline as well as determining all the B-cells

Next consider the point location problem by lemma 5(a), we can use binary search to decide if a query point p lies in the beachhead in $O(\log(n))$ time It is slightly more involved to locate the B-cell containing p in the beachhead

Recall that $Vor(Q) \cap B$ is composed of a collection of free trees with leaves on the beachline and perhaps one on L. We can assign a root to each such free tree: if it reaches L, let its root be the vertex connected to L, otherwise, let its root be the highest leaf vertex, say All the edges then can be directed towards the root using a trick of Tarjan and Vishkin's (1985) form an eulerian directed path beginning at the root and visiting each edge twice, in which case v is an ancestor of w if and only if v is first visited before w and last visited after w; thus the edges can be directed using list ranking We can form regions R_T that enclose each individual tree T If T reaches the line L then the region R_T has three corners formed from the root of the tree and the two extreme leaves of the tree If T does not reach L then let u and v be its top and bottom intersections with the beachline The line joining these two points cannot be crossed by any edge of T since such an edge would have to cross the boundary of B in L or outside the range of these points; hence all of T is to the right of this line and we define R_T as that region of B to the right of this line in this case (Unbounded regions raise a few special cases which are easily dealt with) Each connected region of the beachhead exterior to all the regions R_T belong to a unique B-cell. Thus using binary search we can determine the region R_T (if any) that contains the query point p. If p lies outside all the R_T then we are done Otherwise, we use the same technique as for point location in an e-promontory. Q E D

We are now ready to give the overall algorithm in five steps (A)-(F) Step (A) is done once and the rest are recursively called The complexity $O(\log^2(n))$ follows since steps (B)-(F) each take $O(\log(n))$

(A) First sort S according to its x-coordinate (an $O(\log^2(n))$ sorting method is enough here) Steps (B)-(F) involve partitioning S evenly into $P \cup Q$ (using a vertical line L) and recursively computing $Vor(P)$, $Vor(Q)$ and also the convex hulls $H(P)$, $H(Q)$.

(B) Construct the beachline for Q and the corresponding search structure for point location within the beachhead Similarly, construct the data structure for point location within each strip emanating from the convex hull of Q This takes $O(\log(n))$ time with n processors Do the same for P

(C) For each point v bounding a semiedge of $Vor(P)$ determine whether it lies closer to Q than to P, using the two techniques shown above if v lies to the left of L, determine the sector (strip or slice) containing v and if a strip, do a point location to determine the cell containing v If v lies to the right of L then we check if v lies within the beachhead, and if not we know that v is closer to Q than to P Otherwise, we locate the cell containing v In either case, we can decide if v is closer to Q than to P This can be accomplished in $O(\log(n))$ time with one processor per vertex Repeat the step with the roles of P and Q reversed

(D) At this point we know which semiedges of $Vor(P)$ (and by a symmetrical operation, $Vor(Q)$) meet the contour Using this information, we shall next compute a linear sequence of triangular subcells of cells of $Vor(P)$, whose union covers the contour and such that the contour visits each triangular subcell exactly once, and visits the cells in the given linear order We call this structure the P-conduit The contour will finally be determined by combining the P-conduit with the Q-conduit

(a merging process)

It will simplify things if all the geometric constructions are bounded This can be ensured by finding a rectangle which contains on its inside all points in S, and also the top and bottom contour vertices Since the beachlines on both sides are enclosed by the vertical sides of such a rectangle, we conclude that the contour can only cross its horizontal sides, and no essential information is lost In our discussion of the conduits we shall assume that all the cells and edges are bounded, having been 'clipped' to lie inside this rectangle It is relatively easy to construct such a rectangle in logarithmic parallel time Details are left to the interested reader.

Consider a relevant point p of P, i e , one whose cell meets the contour The contour first enters the p-cell (in $Vor(P)$, perhaps clipped) through an upper semiedge, possibly leaves and returns by several pairs of semiedges (each pair being two halves of the same edge), and finally leaves the cell for ever The direction of travel within the p-cell is clockwise around p and all parts of the contour within the cell are, of course, visible from p. Let e and f be a contiguous pair of semiedges in this clockwise sequence where e is an 'entering' semiedge and f a 'leaving' semiedge Consider these two semiedges together with the list of all edges bounding the (clipped) p-cell included between them in clockwise order around p. Connecting the endpoints in this ordered list of edges to p (including e and f), we obtain an ordered list of triangles with the property that the contour enters the first and leaves the last (to enter a different cell) and enters and leaves each intermediate triangle exactly once This list of triangles forms part of the P-conduit mentioned above It is relatively straightforward to combine all these lists together for all relevant points p, in the appropriate linear sequence, by assigning the appropriate number of processors to each point p namely, one to each edge of the clipped p-cell, thereby locating, counting, and sequencing the lists of triangles around p to link these lists together in the correct way is easily done using one processor per semi-edge The time to do this is $O(\log(n))$ Thus the P-conduit can be formed as a linked list and we can use list-ranking to store an appropriate representation of this structure in an indexed array

(E) Finally we construct the contour by merging the P-conduit with the Q-conduit Say that two triangles T_P and T_Q from the respective conduits *interact* if the bisector separating the respective points p and q (apexes of the respective triangles) meets the intersection of the two triangles Clearly, these triangles interact if and only if the contour contains an edge separating the two points and this edge intersects the common intersection of both triangles Each conduit triangle interacts with at least one on the other side. Thus the contour can be constructed as follows Let T' be the median triangle in the Q-conduit Assigning one processor to each triangle in the P-conduit one can identify the set S of all triangles in the P-conduit which interact with T' This set is an interval of one or more contiguous triangles in the P-conduit, let T_1 and T_2 be the first and last in the list (these may be the same triangle) Then only T_1 and the triangles above it in the P-conduit can interact with triangles above T' in the Q-conduit, with a corresponding observation connecting T_2 with the triangles below T' Thus all pairs of interacting triangles can be identified recursively in $O(\log(n))$ parallel steps Using this information it is straightforward to finish constructing the contour in logarithmic parallel time

(F) Finally construct the cells of $Vor(S)$ by fixing up the cells of $Vor(P), Vor(Q)$ as appropriate

5. Intersections, Partitions, and Related Problems

We consider the following problems: (i) detecting whether a collection of line segments contains any intersection, (ii) triangulating a simple polygon, (iii) balanced recursive partition of a polygon (so the structure of the partition is a logarithmic depth binary tree), and (iv) computing an optimal placement of watchguards in an art gallery. We prove:

Theorem 7. *The above problems (i)-(iv) are all in $NC_T^*(n \log(n))$. For problems (iii) and (iv), if we begin with a triangulated polygon (or art gallery), then the problem in in $NC_T^*(n)$.*

Note that using straightforward emulation [Brent (1974)], the $NC_T^*(n \log(n))$ algorithms above can be converted into $NC_2^*(n)$-solutions. These time-bounds have recently been improved to $O(\log(n))$ [Atallah and Goodrich (1986), Atallah, Cole, and Goodrich (1987)].

The solutions to all these problems share a common basis, which is the construction of the so-called *(vertical) trapezoidal map* of a set of line segments. Let V be a collection of n lines segments, no two of which intersect except perhaps at their endpoints. Following [Lipski and Preparata (1981)] we define the trapezoidal map of V as follows: for each endpoint p of a segment in V, let L_p denote the maximal vertical line segment through p that does not *intersect properly* any segment of V. (We say that two segments intersect properly if their relative interiors intersect.) As is apparent from the illustration in Figure 5, the finite regions of the trapezoidal map are trapezoids.

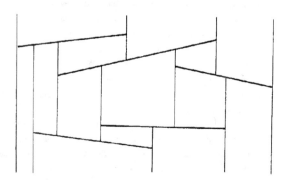

Figure 5. Trapezoidal map

It is natural to combine the problem of segment intersection with the problem of computing the trapezoidal map: we will give an algorithm that on input V, detects if there are intersections among the segments of v and if not, it computes the trapezoidal map of V. For brevity in exposition, we assume no two end points have the same x-coordinate and in particular no segment of V is vertical.

Let T be the segment tree associated with the projection of V on the x-axis [Bentley (1977), Bentley and Wood (1980)]. Recall that T is a balanced binary tree of $2n+1$ leaves. For each k between 1 and $2n+1$, the kth leaf of T from the left is associated with a *canonical interval* on the x-axis: this interval is delimited by the kth smallest x-coordinate in V and the $(k+1)$st smallest one. Similarly, the *canonical interval* of every internal node of T is defined recursively as the union of its two children's canonical intervals. Let $s_1,\ \ldots, s_n$ be the segments of V. Each node v of the segment tree is assigned a set of indices, $L(v)$, called its *node-set* as follows: let $I(s_i)$ be the projection of segment s_i on the x-axis. We say that a node of T *covers* $I(s_i)$ if its canonical interval is contained in $I(s_i)$ but the canonical interval of its father is not contained in $I(s_i)$ (or else the node has no father). We define the node-set $L(v)$ of v to be the set of all indices i such that v covers $I(s_i)$. It is straightforward to see that each index appears in $\leq 2\log(n)$ nodes (at most two nodes per level) and thus that the storage requirement of the segment tree is $O(n\log(n))$.

Let us return to our original problem. Define the *canonical strip* of a node v of T to be the infinite vertical slab formed by the Cartesian product of its canonical interval and $(-\infty, +\infty)$. The intersection of the strip with the segments of V whose indices are in $L(v)$ forms the so-called *hammock* of v, denoted $H(v)$ [Chazelle (1986)]. If V is free of proper intersections then the hammock consists of noncrossing line segments joining two vertical lines. For each node v, define the set $W(v)$ to consist of segments of the form $s \cap S_v$ where S_v is the canonical strip of v and s intersects the interior of S_v and s has at least one endpoint in the closure of S_v. Again, note that each s occurs in at most $2\log(n)$ sets $W(v)$.

First we consider the main idea of the algorithm. The problem of constructing the trapezoidal map of V amounts to computing the segment immediately above (below) each endpoint in V. We can detect if the segments in $H(v)$ intersect by sorting the segments in $H(v)$ in two ways: once according to their left endpoint and once according to their right endpoint. (The endpoints lie, respectively, on the left and right boundaries of the canonical strip.) If these sorting orders disagree, we at once detect intersection. Otherwise, for each segment s of $W(v)$, we can insert s into the linearly ordered *cells* of the canonical strip of v in two ways: by inserting s according to its two endpoints. Again, $s \in W(v)$ intersects some edge in $H(v)$ if and only if the two cells obtained by both ways of inserting s into the canonical strip are the same. If these two tests for $H(v)$ and $W(v)$ pass successfully for each v, then we can conclude that the segments in V do not intersect (see [Chazelle (1986)] for a proof). Note that it is insufficient to just do these tests for $H(v)$.

Now we give some of the details related to sorting. The tree I as well as the canonical intervals can be computed in $O(\log(n))$ time, using sorting on n processors. Next we assign one processor to each segment of V and compute the nodes of T covering each segment in $O(\log(n))$ time (using binary search in the tree). At this point we can assume that we have one list of size $O(n\log(n))$, each list item containing a pair of the form

$$(i,v) = (segment\ index,\ covering\ node)$$

By sorting the pairs (i,v) lexicographically so that v is most important, we get the pairs having a common v into consecutive locations of an array. We may regard the consecutive locations as sublists of pairs corresponding to the set above $H(v)$. We may sort the edges of $H(v)$ in the two ways described above and verify that no intersection occurs. Next, the sets $W(v)$ are similarly constructed with $n\log(n)$ processors in logarithmic time. We may then insert each segment s of $W(v)$ into the sorted sublists of $H(v)$; again we do this in two ways and with $O(n\log(n))$ processors and logarithmic time. So now, we may assume that we have the quadruples

$$(p,v,s_1,s_2)$$

where p is an endpoint of some segment s in V, $W(v)$ contains a portion of the segment s which terminates in p, and finally, the segment s_1 (resp s_2) come from the hammock edges directly above (resp below) p in the canonical strip We sort again to collect in consecutive locations the quadruples involving a fixed endpoint p. By computing the minimum distance among the s_1 (resp s_2) from p, we obtain the edge of V directly above (resp below) p This completes our algorithm for the trapezoidal map To prove that the algorithm is correct, it suffices to observe that by finding the segment immediately above (resp below) an endpoint p will necessarily contribute a hammock edge which lies immediately above (or below) the endpoint in question

Note that the data structure can be used for planar point location Better yet, it allows us to determine the segment immediately above a query point in $O(\log^2(n))$ time, using $O(n \log(n))$ space

In the next two subsections, we show two applications of the trapezoidal map

5.1. Triangulating a Simple Polygon

To triangulate a simple n-gon P, we first compute its trapezoidal map. We follow [Chazelle and Incerpi (1984)] in the following Our goal is to first partition P into monotone polygons To do this, at each reflex corner c that lies in the relative interior of a vertical edge of a trapezoid, we introduce a diagonal edge from c to the corner of P on the opposite vertical edge Such diagonals can be constructed in constant time This now partitions P into a collection of horizontally monotone polygons. A horizotally monotone polygon consists of an *upper* and a *lower chain* of edges, which meet at the two extremal (leftmost, rightmost) corners A chain (upper or lower) is *trivial* if it consists of a single edge

Figure 6 Horizontally monotone polygon with trivial upper chain

We show how to partition a horizontally monotone polygon Q into horizontally monotone subpolygons with a trivial upper or trivial lower chain, as follows Allocate one processor to each edge e of Q By symmetry, assume that e forms the trivial upper chain If the region of the plane sufficiently close to e and below e is outside polygon P then do nothing Otherwise, denoting by u_L and u_R the left and right endpoints of e, we (conceptually) drop the vertical line segments from u_L and u_R (resp) to the boundary of P Let these line segments meet the boundary of P at v_L and v_R, respectively (If e is the leftmost (resp rightmost) edge of its upper chain then $u_L = v_L$ (resp $u_R = v_R$).) Introduce diagonals from u_L (u_R) to the leftmost (rightmost) vertex of P between v_L and v_R Compressing the vertices of each monotone polygon into a single array by parallel prefix, this produces the desired partition of Q in $O(\log(n))$ time using q processors, where q denotes the number of vertices of Q (Figure 6).

So now we may assume that $Q = \{w_1, \ldots, w_q\}$ is a horizontally monotone polygon with a trivial upper chain $w_1 w_q$, and lower chain given by the polygonal line $w_1, \ldots, w_q$. We break up the lower chain into $\sqrt{n}$ contiguous segments of equal size and compute the *upper hull* of each piece (that is, the upper chain of their convex hull). This is similar to our convex hull algorithm in section 3. These hulls form a continuous path that partition Q into a connected upper portion adjacent to $w_1 w_q$ and at least $\sqrt{n}$ portions below the hulls. Then we recursively triangulate the parts of Q below each upper hull (Figure 7).

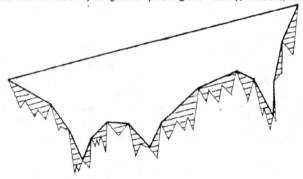

Figure 7. Recursively triangulate below each of the $\sqrt{n}$ upper hulls

As in the analysis in Section 3, if we can triangulate the part of Q above these upper hulls in $O(\log q)$ time using $O(q)$ processors then the complete triangulation of Q will have the same asymptotic complexity. Once again by assigning one processor per pair of upper hulls we can compute all pairwise tangents in logarithmic time (see Section 3). Next we build up a partial triangulation of the region of Q between these upper hulls and the trivial upper chain: 1) pair up consecutive upper hulls (the first and second, the third and fifth, etc.) and for each pair determine the unique tangent between the two upper hulls, adding it into the triangulation; 2) iterate on this process until there is only one upper hull left. Step (1) can be implemented in constant time: to see this, assign one processor per vertex, per current upper hull and per precomputed tangent. At the beginning of each new iteration we assume that the processors assigned to vertices which are no longer on the current upper hulls are de-activated. Then in $O(1)$ time the vertices of the current upper hulls are each labelled with a i.d. number unique to the hull. In this way each (tangent) processor can then decide immediately if it is relevant, that is, if it connects two hulls in a given pair. If so, then the tangent is added into the triangulation and the processor of every vertex lying strictly below the tangent is de-activated. Tangents which crosses the newly added edges of the triangulation also have their processors de-activated. The iteration can then proceed. When the iterations terminate we have the situation of figure 8.

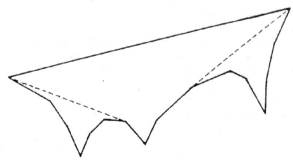

Figure 8. Partial triangulation of region above the upper hulls

It is easy to see that the partial triangulation leaves behind polygonal regions with very simple characteristics: such polygons $Q' = \{u_1, \ldots, u_k\}$ are horizontally monotone with a trivial upper chain $u_1 u_k$, and there is a unique lowest vertex u_l ($1 \le l \le k$) such that the y-coordinate of u_i is decreasing as i increases from 1 to l, and the increasing as i increases from l to k. Furthermore, the subpolygons $\{u_1, \ldots, u_l\}$ and $\{u_l, \ldots, u_k\}$ are also horizontally monotone with a trivial lower chains $u_1 u_l$ and $u_l u_k$, respectively (Figure 9). Since they are also convex, it is now an easy exercise to triangulate each Q' using k processors and $O(\log(k))$ time.

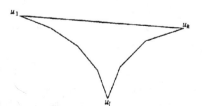

Figure 9. Special monotonic polygons after partial triangulation

In conclusion, we have given a algorithm for triangulating a simple n-gon in $O(\log(n))$ time, using n processors if the vertical trapezoidal map is available, or using $O(n \log(n))$ processors otherwise.

5.2. Polygon-Cutting, Recursive Decompositions and Applications

The polygon-cutting theorem states that any simple polygon has a diagonal which *cuts* it into two roughly equal pieces. In its simplest form, it says that an n-gon can always be cut up into polygons of at most $2(n/3)+1$ vertices. As was shown in [Chazelle (1982)] this property, though quite simple, is of great importance, because like other separator theorems it sets the stage for divide-and-conquer algorithms. We will illustrate this with the problem of placing guards in an art gallery. First we review how the polygon-cutting theorem is used.

In many problems on simple polygons, it is useful to divide a polygon roughly evenly for separate processing, and to recursively proceed. This amounts to constructing a 'decomposition tree' that is balanced (i.e. logarithmic depth), where each node v stores a diagonal of the polygon (representing a partition) and the left and right subtrees below v represent the two polygons defined by this partition; the leaves represent triangles Note that the set of all diagonals stored in the decomposition tree forms a triangulation of the polygon The polygon-cutting theorem implies the converse every triangulation can be organized into a balanced decomposition tree The graph-theoretic dual of the triangulation is a tree whose nodes and edges are in bijective correspondence with the triangles and the diagonals, respectively If a diagonal partitions the boundary of P into two polygonal lines of respectively p and $n-p$ edges then removing the corresponding edge from the tree will leave two trees of respectively $p-1$ and $n-p-1$ nodes What is now needed is an efficient parallel algorithm for computing the size of the subtrees adjacent to every edge in the tree This can be reduced to computing the number of descendents of every node in a rooted tree, which we have already used in our algorithm for Voronoi diagrams (section 4) From this we conclude that balanced decomposition trees can be implemented in $NC\substack{*\\1}(n)$ if the polygon is already triangulated, and in $NC\substack{*\\1}(n\log(n))$ otherwise

In [Chvátal (1975)] it is shown that as long as P is simple it is always possible to place $\lfloor n/3 \rfloor$ watch-guards inside P to keep the whole polygon ('art gallery') in check This means that with $\lfloor n/3 \rfloor$ carefully chosen points every point in P is visible from at least one of the chosen points A simple proof follows from the property that any triangulation of P is 3-colorable. Being a tree, the dual graph of a triangulation of P has at least one leaf This means that if P has more than three vertices, its triangulation contains at least one triangle abc adjacent to the rest of P through ab only Removing this triangle allows us to 3-color the remainder recursively, which then leaves one color available for vertex c A solution to the art-gallery problem then results from placing a guard at each vertex colored with the least-used color

To overcome the inherently sequential nature of this algorithm, we first assume that a decomposition tree T for the polygon is available Our goal is to 3-color a simple polygon P A 3-coloring of P is represented by storing at each edge of T a permutation of the colors c_1, c_2, c_3, and at the leaves of T, an arbitrary 3-coloring of the vertices of the triangle Note that a vertex of P may appear in more than one triangle but we make no assumption that the color assigned to its various appearances at the leaves are consistent The consistency question is resolved by the permutations at the edges Let us describe how the color of any vertex v of P is obtained in this coding scheme Say v appears in the triangle at a leaf l of the decomposition tree T If v is 'locally' assigned a color c at l, then the color of v in the 'global coloring' is obtained by applying the permutations found along the path from l to the root of T We must ensure consistency, i e , different leaves containing v will lead to the same global color for v This is simple. Let us say that a node u of T is *globally consistent* if for all vertices v of P, whenever two leaves below u assigns local colors to v, then the path from these two leaves to u will assign the same global color to v Assume that all nodes at distance greater than k from the root are globally consistent. Let u be a node at distance k from the root, and u_L, u_R be the two children of u It is easy to assign permutations to the two edges from u to its children so that u is globally consistent. (To see this, not that the possible cause for inconsistency is at the two vertices incident to the diagonal of P at u) Starting from the nodes furthest away from the root in $O(\log(n))$ steps, we can compute the permutations In another $O(\log(n))$ steps, with one processor per leaf of T, we can assign the global color to each v in P

6 Polygon Optimization using a Back-and-Forth technique

There has been considerable interest recently in optimization problems where the solution space is a suitable class of polygons (see [Chang (1986)]) One such class of problems is the following, for fixed

$k \geq 3$. Given a convex n-gon P, determine the minimum-area (resp. maximum-area) k-gon that circumscribes (resp. is inscribed in) P. First consider the circumscribing problem. In the sequential setting, [O'Rourke et al (1985)] give a linear time algorithm for $k = 3$ while [Aggarwal,Chang & Yap (1985), Chang(1986)] give an $O(n^2 \log(n) \log(k))$ algorithm for $k \geq 4$. Recently, a factor of $\log(n)$ has been shaved off this result using a general technique in [Aggarwal, Klawe, Moran, Shor & Wilber (1986)]. Since the solution for $k \geq 4$ is at least quadratic time, we cannot have an $NC_k^*(n)$ solution without improving the sequential result. Thus we focus on the minimum circumscribing triangle problem. Our main result is given next: the stated runtime is achieved using what we have dubbed 'back-and-forth subdivision,' a technique new in computational geometry.

Theorem 8. *The problem of computing a minimum circumscribing triangle for a convex n-gon is in* $NC_1^*(n)$.

For convenience we refer to the n edges of a given convex polygon P by their indices in clockwise order from 0 to $n-1$. Also, given an edge i, we denote by $\alpha(i)$ the last edge in clockwise order from i which forms a positive angle with the line through i: put another way, $\alpha(i)$ is the unique edge such that its second terminal (in clockwise order) supports the tangent to P parallel to i and opposite i (there is an easy special case when this tangent lies along an edge). We exhibit a $\sqrt{n}$ divide and conquer strategy (cf. Section 3) which relies on the following geometric characterization developed in [Klee and Laskowski (1985), O'Rourke et al (1985)].

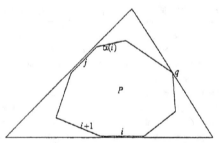

Figure 10. The edges $\{i, i+1, \ldots, \alpha(i)\}$ of P and $T(i,j)$.

We use the following known properties:

(i)   Among the minimum circumscribing triangles of P, at least one such triangle has two of its sides 'flush' (where a side is flush if it lies along an edge of P).

(ii) The midpoint of each side of any minimum circumscribing triangle of P must touch P.

(iii) Given i and j, where $i \leq j \leq \alpha(i)$, let $T(i, j)$ denote the triangle with two sides flush with i and j such that the third side has its midpoint q touching P and such that i, j and q occur in clockwise order on the boundary of P. We write $m(i,j)$ for the edge of P that touches q. In general the third side of $T(i,j)$ is not flush so there will be two choices for $m(i,j)$; we will conventionally choose the larger index (mod n). For each i, there are at most two indices $j^*(i)$ such that the midpoint of the second side of $T(i, j^*(i))$ (i.e., the side that is flush with $j^*(i)$) actually touches P. If there are two choices for $j^*(\iota)$, we choose the edge that has the larger index (mod n) Let $m^*(\iota)$ refer to the edge $m(\iota, j^*(\iota))$, and $T^*(\iota)$ refer to $T(\iota, j^*(\iota))$ We say edge $j^*(\iota)$ (resp $m^*(\iota)$) is *left critical* (resp *right critical*) with respect to ι We will call triangle $T^*(\iota)$ a *locally minimum* triangle with respect to edge ι Note that the midpoint of the edge of $T^*(\iota)$ flush with ι need not touch P

(iv) Monotonicity property An edge $j \in P$ ($\iota \neq j$) is called *low* (*high*, resp) with respect to ι if j precedes $j^*(\iota)$ (j succeeds $j^*(\iota)$, resp) in a clockwise traversal of P By definition then, for each ι, the sequence of edges $(\iota, \iota+1, \quad, \alpha(\iota))$ consists of a sequence of low edges, followed by a left critical edge, followed by a sequence high edges The monotonicity property is as follows Suppose that p is the midpoint of the side of $T(\iota, j)$ lying along j and p is not on ι if p and the side containing ι are on the same side of j then j is high, and if they are on opposite sides then j is low, with respect to ι (Note that this deduction is made without knowledge of the left or right critical edges of ι)

(v) Interspersing property If $\iota \leq \iota'$ then $j^*(\iota) \leq j^*(\iota')$ and $m^*(\iota) \leq m^*(\iota')$

Property (v) is a weakened form of that derived by O'Rourke et al (1986) but is sufficient for our purposes Given ι and j one can compute $m^*(\iota, j)$ using binary search in logarithmic serial time, thus, given ι, the monotonicity property lets us use binary search to compute $j^*(\iota)$ in $O(\log^2(n))$ serial time Thus n processors can compute the locally minimum triangles $T^*(\iota)$ for each ι By property (i), the globally minimum triangle will be found among these $T^*(\iota)$ This can be found in $O(\log(n))$ further steps We shall see that this can be improved to yield an $O(\log(n))$ parallel algorithm using what we shall call 'back-and-forth subdivision '

We define partial right inverses for the two functions j^* and m^* $j^{-1}(k)$ is the unique ι such that $j^*(\iota-1) < k \leq j^*(\iota)$ (in clockwise order), $m^{-1}(k)$ is defined the same way (The functions j^* and m^* are not usually bijective, but if k is in the range of j^* then $j^*(j^{-1}(k))=k$, similarly for m^{-1}) The monotonicity property (iv) shows that these quantities are well-defined and furthermore, given an interval I of length s containing $j^{-1}(k)$, if $j^*(\iota)$ is known for all ι in that interval, then a single processor can compute $j^{-1}(k)$ in $O(\log(s))$ time The idea is that we shall compute approximate values for functions j^* and m^* and for their inverse functions j^{-1} and m^{-1} We can refine an estimate of $j^*(\iota)$ by using information about j^{-1} and m^* and performing binary search in the interval known to contain the true value The other approximations can be refined simultaneously Repeating this process sufficiently often, namely, $\log\log(n)$ times, we compute all these functions exactly A single phase of the process involves knowing for each k an interval $a \quad b$ of length s, say, such that $a < j^{-1}(k) \leq b$. In this case we say that the interval $[a,b]$ *brackets* $j^*(k)$ Using sufficiently many processors (n overall), we can improve this estimate to an interval of length $\sqrt{s}$ the same goes for calculating estimates of the other functions The phase takes $O(\log(s))$ parallel steps

For simplicity we shall assume that n is a power of two We initially choose s as the maximum integer $\leq n$ of the form

$$2^{2^\iota}$$

where ι is an integer, (specifically $\iota = \lfloor \log_2(\log_2(n)) \rfloor$) This avoids rounding difficulties This initial value of s lies between $\sqrt{n}$ and n

Lemma 9. *Let s be a perfect square perfectly dividing n (which is assumed to be a power of 2) For $0 \leq \iota \leq n/\sqrt{s}-1$ let s_ι be the $\iota\sqrt{s}$-th edge in clockwise order around the polygon P Suppose that to each k is* *associated four intervals $J^*(k)$, $J^{-1}(k)$ $M^*(k)$, and $M^{-1}(k)$ respectively bracketing $J^*(k)$, $J^{-1}(k)$, $m^*(k)$, and $m^{-1}(k)$, where each interval is of the form $[s_i\sqrt{s}, s_{(i+1)}\sqrt{s}]$ In other words, the given bracketing intervals are of length $s+1$ and their boundaries are multiples of s Then with n processors all of these intervals can be reduced to intervals of the form $[s_i, s_{i+1}]$, in $O(\log(s))$ parallel steps*

Proof. For $0\leq i < n/\sqrt{s}$ we assign $\sqrt{s}$ processors to compute in $O(\log(s))$ parallel steps the correct subinterval $[s_i, s_{i+1}]$ of $J^*(s_i)$ bracketing $J^*(s_i)$ The i-th processor uses binary search on $M^*(s_i)$ to determine whether $s_i \leq J^*(s_i)$, i e , to determine whether s_i is low, critical, or high with respect to s_i Thus the correct interval bracketing $J^*(s_i)$ is located Reassigning the given processors to this interval $J^*(s_i)$ is computed exactly This exact information about $J^*(s_i)$ at these $n/\sqrt{s}$ sample sides s_i enables us to bracket $J^{-1}(k)$ for *all* sides k of P, since

$$s_i < J^{-1}(k) \leq s_{i+1}$$
if and only if
$$J^*(s_i) < k \leq J^*(s_{i+1}),$$

so this can be checked in time $O(\log(s))$ with one processor reassigned to each edge k, using binary search on the subsequence of edges s_i contained in the interval $J^{-1}(k)$ ($J^*(s_i)$ is known exactly for all i)

Thus we have $J^*(s_i)$ computed for all i and $J^{-1}(k)$ correctly bracketed for all k Next for each sample side s_k we assign $\sqrt{s}$ processors one is assigned to each side i in the interval $J^{-1}(k)$ (which is now of the form $[s_i, s_{i+1}]$) The processor assigned to i queries $M^*(i)$ and determines whether k is low, critical, or high with respect to i By the monotonicity property this enables $J^{-1}(s_k)$ to be determined exactly. When this computation is finished, $J^*(i)$ can be recomputed for *every* edge i just as $J^{-1}(i)$ was computed The refinement of our estimates of $M^*(k)$ and $M^{-1}(k)$ is achieved by symmetric methods. Q.E D

The initial conditions for applying the lemma are slightly different since in general $n>s$. The aim then is to achieve initial bracketing intervals of length s however, essentially the same ideas apply Repeating the refinement phase $\log\log(n)$ times all quantities are computed exactly Notice that since all the tasks assigned involve easily-computed subsequences and subintervals of $0 \cdots n-1$, processor assignment presents no difficulty in this algorithm, It is clear that this method takes overall parallel time

$$\sum_k O(\log(n^{2^{-k}})) = \sum_k O(\frac{\log(n)}{2^k}) = O(\log(n))$$

Additional Remarks. Boyce et al (1985) have shown that some of the properties similar to those given for the minimum circumscribing triangle also hold for the maximum inscribed triangle It is not clear if the back-and-forth technique can be extended here since the monotonicity property (iv) is not available However an $O(\log^2(n))$ solution is possible For the dual problem of computing the maximum inscribed triangle, simple divide and conquer gives a solution using $O(\log^2(n))$ time and n processors In fact, unlike the minimum circumscribed k-gons (for $k\geq 4$), such a divide and conquer technique yields an $O(k\log^2(n))$ time for computing a maximum inscribed k-gon using n processors Finally, Toussaint (1983) has shown that the minimum circumscribing rectangle for a given convex n-gon can be found in $O(n)$ sequential time. Using the geometric characterization given by Freeman and Shapira (1975), it is easy to compute such a rectangle in $O(\log(n))$ time using only $n/\log(n)$ processors

In fact, the diameter of a convex polygon can also be computed in $O(\log(n))$ time using $n/\log(n)$

processors, as the following brief outline suggests If we can compute for each i its antipodal vertex $\delta(i)$ (the endpoint of $\alpha(i)$) it is straightforward to compute the distance of $\delta(i)$ from the line through i for each i, and then compute the minimum of all these distances with the stated resources We take $n/\log(n)$ processors and assign each processor to a group of $\log(n)$ successive sides of the polygon Each processor first computes the antipodal vertex for the first side in its alotted group (this involves unimodular search in logarithmic serial time), and then begins to scan in a clockwise direction along its group of sides Its 'primary task' is to compute $\delta(i)$ for all sides within this group Going from side i to $i+1$, the corresponding antipodal vertex may either remain the same, increase by 1, or increase by more than 1 In the latter case the gap between $\delta(i)$ and $\delta(i+1)$ could be considerably more than $\log(n)$, and the processor might not achieve its primary task. However, in this case, if k denotes the side beginning at $\delta(i)$, we know that $\delta(k)$ is the vertex ending the i-th edge. Thus the processor can begin a 'secondary task,' namely computing $\delta(j)$ for $j=k,k+1,\quad$ until it either reaches the end of the group containing k or $\delta(j)$ increases, in which case it can determine $\delta(i+1)$ and revert to its primary task It is easy to show that, for every i, $\delta(i)$ is computed by some processor, either as a primary or secondary task.

7   Convex hull in 3 dimensions and related structures.

In this section we shall discuss the problem of computing the convex hull $H(S)$ of a set S of points in three dimensional space The method originally described in the FOCS paper ran in parallel time $O(\log^4(n))$, but the method to be presented here is in $NC_3^+(n)$ Thus we now match the asymptotic efficiency of Anita Chow's method [1980], and we do not need an optimal parallel sorting algorithm As with the 2-dimensional Voronoi diagram problem the algorithm is based on a serial divide-and-conquer technique already known in the literature We shall employ a new data-structure, which has independent interest, to solve queries of the following kind given a line L and a polytope K, to determine whether L intersects K and if not to return a plane through L tangent to K Such queries will be called *line-queries*, they will be discussed in detail later Let us state the main result of this section

Theorem 10 *There is an $NC_3^+(n)$ algorithm for constructing the convex hull $H(S)$ of a set S of n points in 3-space, which only uses sorting at a preprocessing stage and hence can use any sorting algorithm in $NC_3^+(n)$ or better The algorithm produces as a by-product a data-structure suitable for answering line-queries about $H(S)$ in serial time $O(\log^2(n))$*

Recall the serial divide-and-conquer algorithm [Preparata and Hong (1977)] to compute the convex hull of S the set of points S is evenly split into two sets by a horizontal plane R, which does not contain any point in S, Let P and Q denote the points in S above and below R, respectively Recursively compute $H(P)$ and $H(Q)$, compute the *sleeve* joining the two hulls, i e , the chain of faces tangent to the two hulls and meeting three or more points of S, then merge $H(P)$ with $H(Q)$ along the sleeve to form the convex hull $H(S)$

For the rest of this section R will continue to denote a horizontal plane, which we shall call the *separating plane*, partitioning S into upper and lower parts P and Q respectively Consider that part of the sleeve on and above the separating plane R One might imagine that it was homeomorphic to a cylinder with boundary, but sleeve faces can meet one another above the separating plane, so it can have several holes Each partial sleeve face has an edge contained in R, and two edges incident on this edge, all other edges on this partial face will be called *seam edges* and given a left-to-right (i e , clockwise) orientation These chains of seam edges join together to form what will be called the *upper seam* of the $H(S)$ Thus the upper seam has the form of a directed Eulerian circuit, but vertices may be visited more than once and the same edge of $H(S)$ may occur with both orientations along the seam [4] The same edge e in $H(P)$, say, will be visited in both directions by the seam if both the front and back tangent planes (see Definition 11) through that edge to $H(Q)$ are tangent to $H(P)$, it is easy to construct examples where this happens The *lower seam*, occurring below the separating plane R, is defined similarly

Our algorithm is simple in principle though the development is lengthy it depends on computing the seams efficiently at each stage To compute the upper seam, say, assign one processor to each edge of $H(P)$, to peform what will be called a 'line query,' relative to $H(Q)$ Consider a fixed edge of $H(P)$, let L be the line containing it If the edge belongs to the upper seam it is necessary (a) that L not meet the interior of $H(Q)$, and (b) one (or conceivably both) of the two planes through L tangent to $H(Q)$ should not intersect the interior of $H(P)$ To determine whether a given plane passing through L is tangent to $H(P)$ can be accomplished in constant time by inspecting the two faces of $H(P)$ meeting L

Once the edges in the seam have been calculated, their cyclic connection order can be ascertained in logarithmic time by a list-ranking process The full structure of the sleeve can be deduced once both seams have been constructed by implementing what is essentially a merging process, easily accomplished in logarithmic time Therefore we shall now consider these line queries more closely

Let K be a convex polytope and L an oriented line not meeting the interior of K There are two half-planes through L tangent to K (they bound the convex hull of $L \cup K$ let us ignore the

---

[4] The possibility that the seam can have self-intersections complicates both the sequential algorithm and ours We are indebted to Herbert Edelsbrunner (private communication) for drawing our attention to this possibility

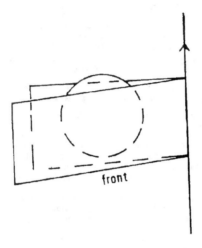

Figure 11: Illustrating the front and back tangent planes

trivial case where K and L are contained in the same plane). It is helpful to distinguish these planes in a canonical way.

Definition 11 *With K and L as above, consider the set of all half-planes bounded by L which intersect K. All such half-planes can be parametrized by a rotational angle θ about L. Assuming that L does not intersect (the interior of) K, these angles θ sweep out an interval $[\theta_0, \theta_1]$ of angles where we can distinguish these two bounding angles (since L is oriented) by requiring that $\theta_1 > \theta_0$ in the anticlockwise sense, and $\theta_1 - \theta_0 \leq \pi$. These bounding angles define the two planes through L tangent to K, and we call the one at angle θ_0 the back tangent-plane to K through L, and the other the front tangent-plane. The line-query for L and K is to determine whether L meets K transversally, and, if not, to compute the front and back tangent planes through L to K.*

If we visualize L and K so that L is in the plane of the page, and oriented upwards, and K is to its left, then the front and back planes will be in front of and behind K respectively (see figure 11).

Setting up the means to solve such queries will occupy most of this section. To begin with, let us consider a rather simple query which we call a *point-query*.

Given a plane T meeting a corner p of a convex polyhedron K, to determine whether T is tangent to K, and if not to give the two faces incident to p which T cuts.

This is solved by providing a *test polygon* at p, namely a polygon which forms the boundary of the region of intersection of a fixed plane M separating p from all the other corners of K. Clearly the plane T cuts K if and only if it cuts this test polygon, and if so then the edges where it cuts the polygon identify the faces incident to p which it cuts. The corners of the test polygon are unimodal with respect to height above (or below) the plane T, so it is easy then to solve the

25

queries in logarithmic serial time by a variant of binary search. The problem, therefore, is to construct a test polygon in parallel, with one processor, say, assigned to each edge of K incident to p. Indeed, it is easy to construct such a polygon once at least one line N has been found which meets the interior of K at p, since then a suitable separating plane normal to this line can be found (take all the projections of the incident edges on N and find the one closest to p in logarithmic time, let r be its distance from p, then choose the plane passing perpendicularly through N at half this distance). To find a line entering K at p, simply choose three corners adjacent to p and let q be their average, then pq defines a suitable line. Summarizing,

Lemma 12 *Given a convex polyhedron K with ℓ corners, it is possible to construct test polygons for each corner in $O(\log(\ell))$ parallel time overall with ℓ processors.*

The following lemma shows where point-queries could arise in constructing the convex hull. Its simple proof is omitted.

Lemma 13 *Let T be a plane which meets the sleeve of $H(S)$ at some corner p but does not intersect any face of the sleeve. Then T can meet the interior of $H(S)$ if and only if it meets the interior at p, and in this case the polygonal region of intersection of T with $H(S)$ is contained in $H(P)$ if p is in the upper seam and in $H(Q)$ if p is in the lower seam.*

The rest of this section is organized as follows. We introduce the notion of 'seam polytope,' and of localizing a query to a sub-polytope. We study the sequencing and nesting properties of the seam on a seam polytope, and use them to give that part of the polytope above the seam the structure of a forest of rooted trees. We introduce the idea of a 'near split' on a polytope which can be used to localize a line-query on the polytope. Next we define the 'core and lobes' of a seam polytope, and show how to localize a line-query to one of these lobes. Next we show how to decompose a lobe recursively by a sequence of near-splits, in a balanced manner, thereby completing the construction for solving line-queries. Finally we show, given a description of a sleeve with its incident edges and faces (in cyclic order), how to build the two associated seam polytopes (a seam polytope is obtained, roughly speaking, by discarding irrelevant faces from $H(S)$. the resulting polytope will only resemble $H(S)$ close to the seam, so it is necessary to build it from scratch).

7.1 Definition and characteristics of a seam polytope

For each of the two seams of the sleeve as considered above we shall construct a 'seam polytope.' a bounded convex polytope which has a distinguished circuit of directed edges, called the seam, matching the corresponding seam of the sleeve.

Definition 14 *A seam polytope is a convex 3-dimensional polytope with two distinguished horizontal faces, the base and the top, and the other faces partitioned into two sets, called, for mnemonic purposes, the green and blue faces respectively. The edges along the top and base are called top and base edges respectively. No green face meets the base and no blue face meets the top. Each blue face meets the base in a proper edge and is either triangular or trapezoidal in shape. The seam vertices and edges are those vertices and edges bounding blue faces but not meeting the base. Edges connecting the seam to the base are called blue edges, and edges meeting only green faces are called green edges, and vertices meeting only green faces are called green vertices.*

To require that the blue faces have at most 4 sides is not essential but simplifies things. it is based on the assumption that the blue faces are formed by intersecting sleeve faces with the halfspace above the separating plane, and that S is in general position so all the faces of $H(S)$ are triangular. From our previous discussion we know that by orienting the blue faces we can describe a circuit of directed edges which includes all seam vertices and edges but can include the same (undirected) edge twice (with both orientations). specifically, when two blue faces meet

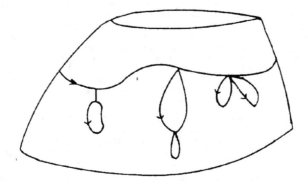

Figure 12: A seam polytope: sea, mainland, islands, peninsulas.

at a seam edge, that edge will be met twice in the directed circuit. Henceforth the *seam* will generally denote the *directed* circuit so formed. It cannot be assumed that every green face meets the top of the seam polytope; moreover, the green faces can have any number of bounding edges, and their connectivity pattern can be complex.

In this section when we speak of connectivity we mean 'face connectivity.' In other words, two blue or green faces are adjacent in this relation if and only if they share an edge: it is not enough that they have a vertex in common. We speak of 'green component' to mean a connected component of the set of green faces in this sense. The set of blue faces is connected, since each face is connected to the base (we visualize it as forming a connected blue 'sea'); There is one green component meeting the top, which will be called the 'mainland.' however, there may be more green 'islands' and 'peninsulas' formed where the seam returns upon itself, and the seam may visit the same edge twice, so both incident faces are blue faces. A green component is a 'peninsula' when it shares a vertex with another component at the point where the seam first meets it. If at the point where the seam first meets it the incoming and outgoing seam edges are coincident (blue) edges, then we think of the component as an island. This distinction helps us to visualize the polytope: it is not important algorithmically. See figure 12.

Let us reconsider briefly the construction of the sleeve and the two seam polytopes that are built during this construction. Without loss of generality we consider only the upper seam. The base of the seam polytope is the intersection of $H(S)$ with the separating plane R. The top of the seam polytope may be defined by a horizontal (parallel to R) plane which passes just above the highest vertex on the upper seam (since the vertices in S can be assumed presorted with respect to the z-coordinate, this vertex can be obtained with little computational overhead.) The planes supporting the faces on the sleeve define the blue faces of the polytope; the planes supporting those faces of $H(S)$ which meet the blue faces above R define the green faces of the seam polytope.

Note. It is significant that the green faces are faces of $H(P)$ and the blue faces are faces of the sleeve, but whereas a part of every sleeve face becomes a blue face of the polytope, only those faces of $H(P)$ incident to the seam from above define green faces of the seam polytope. Therefore the green faces will in general be larger than the corresponding faces of $H(P)$. The advantage is that their interconnection structure is simpler than the structure of $H(P)$ itself.

For the rest of this section, if K is any polytope and A any subset of K, suppose that we have determined for a given line L that if L penetrates K then it penetrates A, and if it does not penetrate K then the front (respectively, back) plane through L to K must coincide with the front (back) plane through L to A. Then we say that the given line-query (for front or back plane) has been *localized to* A. Since the front plane to K through L coincides with the back plane to K through L', where L' is the same line as L with the opposite orientation, we can always restrict our attention to the front plane. (For our purposes A will always be the convex hull of some of the corners of K.)

A hierarchy of seam polytopes can be constructed while $H(S)$ is being built, for any oriented line L, a line-query for $H(S)$ and L can be solved by a recursive sequence of line-queries for L and this hierarchy of seam polytopes, as follows

Lemma 15 *Let $H(S)$ be as defined above and suppose that Π is the seam polytope for its upper seam. Given an oriented line L, suppose that we wish to determine whether L intersects the interior of $H(S)$ and if not to give the front plane through L tangent to $H(S)$. Then a solution to the corresponding question for Π either solves the query for $H(S)$ or localizes it to $H(P)$ or $H(Q)$.*

Proof. First consider the cases where L intersects the boundary of Π at two points. These are either (a) through the base and another face, (b) through a blue face and another face, or (c) through a green face and the top or another green face. Clearly in the first two cases L intersects the interior of $H(S)$ (the base and the blue faces are contained in $H(S)$).

In case (c) let us distinguish three subcases. The first is where L intersects some green face in some green component A, not the mainland, and the other point where L meets the boundary of Π is on another component (perhaps the mainland). For definiteness assume A is an island. Imagine reconstructing that part of the boundary of $H(S)$ contained within the same part of the seam as the island A. This can be done piecemeal by 'shaving' parts off the island (thus introducing planes supporting green faces of $H(S)$ not included in the polytope). When such a new face is created it is easy to see that L continues to intersect the green island (perhaps in the new face) in exactly one point. Repeating this process we eventually obtain a polytope Π' where the island A in Π matches a green island A' in Π' and the latter island exactly matches part of the (green) boundary of $H(S)$. Thus L intersects $H(S)$ in this case. In the second subcase, L intersects two green faces in the same component (perhaps the mainland). We imagine a similar 'shaving' procedure by which we eventually match the appropriate part of the boundary of $H(S)$. This time there are two possibilities: either at the end of the process L is demonstrated to intersect $H(S)$ (in two points in the same component) or at some step the two intersection points are separated from the polytope. At this step the front plane through L tangent to the resulting polytope is tangent to the face just introduced. let Δ be the pyramid just shaved off, so L intersects it but not its base (which is also the new face of the resulting polytope), the polygonal region of intersection of Δ with the given front tangent plane must meet the shaved polytope, so it must meet the new face. While subsequent 'shaving' operations may move the points of contact of the corresponding front planes, they all maintain contact with the same green component. Since this represents a green part of the polytope, it is in $H(P)$ and the query has been localized in both cases to $H(P)$. In the third subcase, the line L penetrates the mainland and the top. this is essentially the same as the second subcase

Next consider the cases where L does not intersect the interior of Π, and so the front plane T through L tangent to Π is well-defined. If T meets Π on the seam, then using a point query we can determine whether it penetrates the interior of $H(S)$ near the point of tangency with Π. If it does not then it solves the query for $H(S)$. Otherwise, it either (d) intersects two faces on the sleeve or (e) intersects two faces of $H(P)$ above the sleeve. In case (d) L intersects $H(S)$, in case (e) either L intersects a face of $H(P)$ or the front plane tangent to $H(P)$ solves the query for $H(S)$

Finally, the point of tangency may be (f) on the top or (g) on the base in which case the query is localized to $H(P)$ or $H(Q)$ respectively Q E D

The following is an immediate corollary

Lemma 16 *Suppose that a hierarchy of seam polytopes have been constructed along with $H(S)$, and that S has size $O(n)$ If auxiliary search structures have been provided which enable the line queries for the seam polytopes to be solved in serial time $O(\log(n))$ then line queries for $H(S)$ can be solved in $O(\log^2(n))$ serial time overall*

We shall next see an appropriate search structure for an individual seam polytope which achieves the time bound in Lemma 15 If an individual seam polytope together with a search structure can be constructed in CREW time $O(\log^2(n))$ with n processors — and it can, as we shall see — then the overall time of $O(\log^3(n))$ for the construction of $H(S)$ is achieved

7.2   Nested structure of seam and bridges

In this section we shall begin analyzing the structure of the seam and the green section of a given seam polytope We aim to identify one or more treelike structures in the set of green edges which will permit us to decompose the polytope in a balanced way in the spirit of Goodrich's improvement to the Voronoi diagram algorithm incorporated into Section 4 As already noted the polytope can be viewed as composed of top, base, a blue sea, and one or more green components, of which one, the mainland, surrounds the top The seam can be represented as a sequence of vertices, possibly with repetitions We can assume that this sequence is stored in an array which we may call the *seam list* We assume that the edge connecting the last vertex on the list to the first is on one of the green faces which reach the top, this implies that it is on the mainland The notion of the span of a vertex will prove useful given any seam vertex v, let i be the first and j the last index where it appears in the seam list Then the interval $[i \quad j]$ is called the *span* of v Among the green edges (edges bounding two green faces) let us call those incident to the top or to the seam *connector edges* If we remove these connector edges, the remaining green edges cannot contain any cycles (otherwise there would be green faces bounded away from the seam), in other words, they form a forest of free trees

Definition 17 *A bridge is either (a) a connector joining two seam vertices or (b) a connector joining the top to the seam or (c) one of the free trees of green edges and vertices together with its incident connectors Bridges of type (a) are called singular bridges, those of type (b) are called trivial, and those of type (c) are called nonsingular*

See figure 13 The following lemma reflects the nesting structure of seam vertices and bridges The first part says that any two seam vertices have disjoint spans or the span of one includes that of the other

Lemma 18 *Given distinct seam vertices v and v' with spans $[i,j]$ and $[i',j']$ respectively, if $i < i' < j$ then $j' < j$ Given any bridge B, either all the seam vertices incident to B have disjoint spans or this holds for all but one of these vertices where the exceptional vertex has a span which includes all the others*

Proof The first part follows from a simple topological argument suppose that the seam visited v at i and j and v' at i' and j' where $i < i' < j < j'$ Then one can argue that the path between i' and j' includes within it (on the 'right-hand side') at least one blue face bounded away from the base Namely, the path from i' to j would have blue faces to its immediate right, so would the path from j to j', therefore the combined path would enclose some blue faces of the polytope, since the seam is bounded away from the base these faces would b $\sim$ ounded away from the base See figure 14

For the second part, define the depth of a seam vertex as follows the seam vertices at depth 0 are those not included in the span of any other vertex, inductively, those at depth $k+1$ are included in the span of vertices of depth k but none at depth $k+1$ A seam vertex is at depth 0 if and only if it is on the mainland Vertices at greater depths are either incident only to blue faces

29

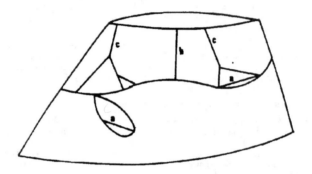

Figure 13: Bridges on a seam polytope.

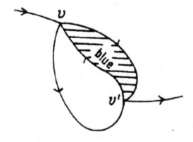

Figure 14: The spans of seam vertices cannot interlace.

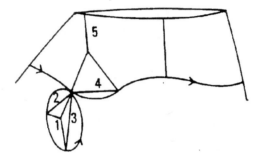

Figure 15: Covering relation: 1 covers 2, 3 covers 1 and 2, 5 covers 4.

or are on green components; all vertices on the same component are at the same depth except for that vertex where the seam first meets the component (and last leaves it). Since clearly all seam vertices incident to the same bridge are on the same component, and all seam vertices at the same depth have disjoint spans, the rest of the lemma follows. Q.E.D.

Next we define the *inner vertex span* of a nontrivial bridge B. Let B be a nontrivial bridge and V the set of seam vertices on B: if all vertices in V have disjoint spans then we define the leftmost (rightmost) seam vertex on B is the vertex in V whose span is leftmost (respectively, rightmost). On the other hand, if some vertex in V has a span including the spans of all others in V then it is defined as the leftmost seam vertex; among the other vertices in V the one whose span is rightmost is defined as the rightmost seam vertex on B. The *inner vertex span* of a nontrivial bridge B is the smallest interval $[i \ldots j]$ where j is the first seam occurrence of its rightmost seam vertex and i the last seam occurrence before j of its leftmost vertex. Note that the span of the bridge B does not necessarily include the spans of its extreme seam vertices but it includes the spans of all other vertices in B. That part of the seam represented by the span we call the *lower path for B*. (Note that we call this a path *for B*; since it follows the seam, it is not a path in B.) There is a unique path in B of green edges, called the *upper path in B*, connecting the extreme vertices such that all vertices in B are contained between the lower path for B and upper path in B. (This will be covered in more detail later.) Combining these two paths (the upper being directed from right to left) we obtain the *circuit around B*. This circuit is not necessarily a simple circuit. The part on it and to its left we consider the interior of the circuit, which it surrounds. Thus all of B is surrounded by this circuit.

Definition 19 *Given two distinct nontrivial bridges B and B', B covers B' if the circuit around B surrounds all of B'.*

See Figure 15. It is clear from the definition that this covering relation is acyclic and irreflexive and can be considered to give the set of bridges the structure of a forest of rooted trees. We define a *principal bridge* to be a nontrivial bridge which is on the mainland and which is covered by no other bridge. Thus a nonsingular principal bridge is one which is connected to the top of the seam polytope. There is at most one connector joining any bridge to the top, because otherwise there would exist a green face bounded away from the seam.

31

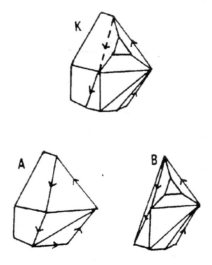

Figure 16: Near-split of a polytope.

We give every bridge a root as follows: in a principal nonsingular bridge, the root is the unique vertex joined to the top. In any other nonsingular bridge the root is on the seam: it is the leftmost vertex on the seam (strictly speaking to avoid ambiguity the root should be associated with the leftmost connector in clockwise order joining this vertex to the bridge). We shall see later that the covering relation among the bridges and the parent relation within them (implicitly fixed by choosing roots for all the bridges considered as trees) can be recovered from information about the order of occurrence of connectors along the seam.

7.3 Near splits, core and lobes of a seam polytope.

The data-structure we shall describe for line-queries will make extensive use of a partition method which we call *near-splitting*. A natural divide-and conquer method to solve a line query for a line L and a polytope K would be to divide K by a plane into two simpler parts: by solving the line-query relative to the face common to the two parts we could localize to one or other part. Since such a splitting face could have a large number of vertices, to localize the query would require logarithmic serial time. Therefore rather than splitting K into two parts meeting at a common face we shall decompose K into two convex polytopes which meet in a set with nonempty interior and whose union is K. This motivates the following definition.

Definition 20 *Let K be a seam polytope, and J a polygonal Jordan curve whose corners are corners of K and whose edges are in the boundary of K (so successive corners of J are always in the same face). Let A be the convex hull of those corners of K on and outside J; let B be the convex hull of those corners of K on and inside J. Then A and B form a near split of the polytope K. See figure 16.*

Lemma 21 *With A, B, J, and K as in the above definition, let L be an oriented line. Then if suitable test polygons are provided for both A and B at each vertex of J, a solution to a line-query*

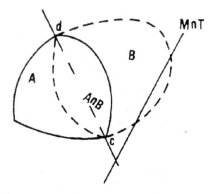

Figure 17: Test polygons help localize the query.

for L relative to $A \cap B$ either solves the line-query for K or can be used with $O(1)$ extra work (on a serial processor) to localize the query to A or B.

Proof. If one imagines A being formed by successively discarding vertices in the boundary of K which are strictly inside J, it is easy to conclude that J is composed of edges and vertices of A and the boundary of A matches that of K outside J and that of $H(J)$ inside J. Let A_1 (respectively, A_2) represent that part of the boundary of A on and outside (respectively, on and inside) J. Similarly, let B_1 (respectively, B_2) represent that part of the boundary of B on and inside (respectively, on and outside) J. Then $A_1 \cup B_2$ is the boundary of K and $B_1 \cup A_2$ is simultaneously the boundary of $H(J)$ and of $A \cap B$. Consequently $A \cup B = K$ and $A \cap B = H(J)$.

Given a line-query for an oriented line L against K, suppose that it has been solved for $A \cap B$. If L penetrates this set then clearly it penetrates K: otherwise, let T be the front tangent plane through L to $A \cap B$. Since this latter set is $H(J)$, T must be tangent to J: suppose that it meets J at some corner p. This is on the boundary of K, and since all of J is on the same side of T, T cannot cut both A and B transversally. Therefore to localize the query it is enough to eliminate one of these polytopes from consideration: With the aid of test polygons this can be done in constant (serial) time without requiring the vertex p to have low degree. To see this, let M be a plane which separates the vertex p from the others in both A and B, so it serves to define test polygons for p relative to $A \cap B$ (and to A and B also). Consider the intersection of M with the boundaries ∂A and ∂B of A and B respectively. (See figure 17). We wish to determine whether the line $M \cap T$ meets $\partial A - \partial(A \cap B)$ or $\partial B - \partial(A \cap B)$ transversally (it cannot meet both transversally). Note that the boundaries of A and B meet at two points c and d of M, and the two given curves lie on opposite sides of the line joining these two points. One of these curves can be eliminated in constant time by considering the relative placements of this line and the line $M \cap T$. Q.E.D.

Now let Π be a seam polytope. We want to supply it with a structure suitable for solving line-queries: the structure will be one which uses 'near splits' recursively to localize the queries. The first step in such a procedure will be to decompose the polytope into a (rather simple) 'core' with some 'lobes' attached.

Definition 22 *A multiple vertex is a seam vertex visited more than once by the seam. A principal bridge is a bridge on the mainland which is covered by no other bridge. Given a*

33

multiple vertex v there exist two base vertices x and y to its left and right respectively and adjacent to it (or at least on blue faces incident to it) such that the Jordan curve through vxy contains exactly that part of the seam within the span of v We define the lobe under v to be the subpolytope formed by all corners on and inside this curve (thus containing the given part of the seam) Let B be a singular principal bridge with two incident seam vertices u and w there exist base vertices x and y such that the Jordan curve $uxyw$ contains on its inside exactly those seam vertices within the span of B The convex hull of all corners on and inside this Jordan curve is the lobe under B Finally suppose that B is a (nontrivial) nonsingular principal bridge, which must therefore have extremal seam vertices u and w and a vertex v adjacent to the top, again there exist base vertices x and y on blue faces incident to u and w respectively such that the Jordan curve $vuxyw$ contains all seam vertices within the span of B on its inside, this curve defines the lobe under B in this case

Given a seam polytope Π, suppose that the following operations are performed

1 For each multiple vertex v on the mainland, a Jordan curve enclosing the lobe under v is chosen as described above, and these Jordan curves are chosen not to cross one another let Π' be the convex hull of all corners on or outside all these Jordan curves We can consider Π' to have been obtained by performing a *lobotomy* at each of these lobes — discarding the vertices inside the given Jordan curves Each new face of Π' may be considered a blue face and the resulting seam polytope has no green components except the mainland

2 For each nontrivial principal bridge on Π' (principal bridges on Π and Π' correspond one-to-one), choose a Jordan curve (with 4 or 5 vertices as appropriate) surrounding the lobe under that bridge and ensure that these Jordan curves do not cross one another let Π'' be the convex hull of all corners of Π' on or outside all of these Jordan curves Thus the lobes under each principal bridge have been removed

3 For the singular bridges, let both new faces created be considered as blue faces, for the nonsingular bridges, it can be deduced from the convexity of Π' that uvw (as discussed in Definition 22) forms a face, which may be considered a green face, and the other two faces may be considered as blue

See figure 18 The polytope Π' is called the *core* of Π This polytope has a rather simple structure, since the only green faces not meeting the top are the triangular faces replacing nonsingular principal bridges All paths from the top to the base not including seam edges contain one blue edge and one or two green edges The following lemma shows how to use near-splits recursively to solve a line query against Π''

Lemma 23 *Suppose that a seam polytope Π is processed as above yielding Π' and then its core Π'' Let L be a fixed oriented line Then in $O(\log(n))$ serial time it can be determined whether L intersects the core, and if not, a line-query for L can be localized to the correct lobe of the polytope Π*

Proof Let p_1 and p_2 be two vertices on the top, connected by edges of the core to vertices q_1 and q_2, respectively, on the base, where these connecting paths do not cross and contain no seam edges (thus they each have at most three edges in them) These can be joined along the top and base to produce a Jordan curve which can then be used to form a near-split of the polytope into sub-polytopes A and B Although these sub-polytopes are not exactly seam polytopes, they retain the important feature that there exist short paths (at most 3 edges) connecting the base to the top Thus this procedure can be repeated in a balanced fashion to solve any line-query against Π'' in logarithmic time Suppose that the line-query has been solved in this way, positively, in the sense that a well-defined front plane T through L tangent to Π'' at some corner x has been found Then x is incident to at most two lobes of Π', and T can meet the interior of at most one hence the line-query can be localized to the correct lobe of Π' using a

34

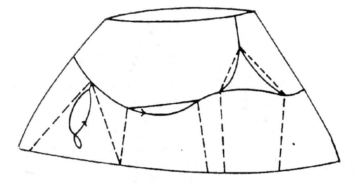

Figure 18: Lobes in a seam polytope.

Next using the structure defined later in this section for searching a lobe, the query can be solved against this lobe. Suppose the query yields a positive answer so another plane tangent to Π' at some corner y of Π' is found. Then y is incident to at most one lobe of Π so the same procedure can be repeated to solve the query against Π, as required. Q.E.D.

7.4 Balanced decomposition of a lobe.

We now show how to decompose a lobe by successive near-splits. Recall that a lobe could have been separated from a seam polytope by a Jordan curve with 3, 4, or 5 vertices. The lobe has essentially the structure itself of a seam polytope except that it does not reach the top and it has one, two, or three 'back faces' respectively forming the back of the convex hull of the 3 to 5 vertices in question. These 'back faces' do not matter in line queries and they need not have any particular color. Also the seam need no longer be a closed circuit, but it inherits the sequencing and nesting structure from the larger polytope, and the concept of bridge still applies. The following rather straightforward lemma describes the basis of the recursive decomposition.

Lemma 24 *Suppose that i and j index vertices along the seam of a lobe Λ and P is a path of edges and vertices from the vertex at j which we shall denote v, say, to that at i (denoted u) where the corners of P are (except at the ends) green vertices and pairs of successive corners belong to the same green face. If u and v are the same vertex we assume that P has length zero. Then P can be continued into a Jordan curve (with one or two more corners on it) in the boundary of Λ such that the green vertices and edges surrounded by J are precisely those surrounded by the seam path from i to j joined to P.*

Proof. Let e be the seam edge $(i-1, i)$ and f the seam edge $(j, j+1)$. Choose a base point x common to the blue face meeting e; similarly choose a base point y on the same blue face as f. (This is ambiguous if and only if e and f are the same edge with opposite orientations, in which case we can choose x and y on the blue faces meeting this edge from the left and right respectively.) Then the path $uxyv$ extends P to a suitable Jordan curve; when u and v are the same this path is triangular. Q.E.D.

Using the hierarchical structure among and within bridges we can obtain a balanced decomposition of the lobe, but a few details remain to be considered first. The structure of bridges will

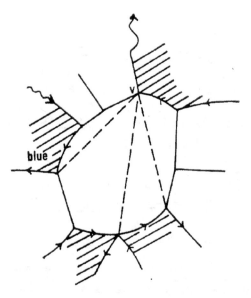

Figure 19: Spanning face: bridges, fictitious green edges.

furnish paths P suitable for applying Lemma 24. As already mentioned this structure will be exploited solely to yield balanced decompositions of a seam polytope or a lobe of a seam polytope. In the absence of multiple seam vertices this structure would furnish us with the decompositions we need (after some effort): however, because the seam can return upon itself there could be many green components consisting of a single green face surrounded by the seam and incident to no bridge whatsoever. To answer this difficulty we shall introduce some 'degenerate' bridges. Let v be a multiple seam vertex and let e and f be the seam edges first entering and last leaving v. If these edges are coincident or else if the two edges e and f bound the same green face on their left, then we regard the vertex v as forming a degenerate bridge whose span is the span of v.

A *spanning face* is a green face which the seam either surrounds completely or meets in a disconnected set of indices.

In the following lemma, recall that the bridges have been given the structure of rooted trees rather than just free trees by making the topmost vertex of principal bridges and the leftmost vertex of other bridges the root. (More precisely, the leftmost connector on these bridges defines the roots.)

Lemma 25 *Let F be a spanning face in the lobe. Then (i) there is a unique vertex v or bridge B whose span includes all other bridges and seam vertices incident to the face; (ii) for every other bridge B' incident to F, its first and last seam vertices are incident to F, and B is the parent of B' in the covering relation (i.e., B covers B' and every other bridge covering B' also covers B); (iii) if B and B' are two bridges such that B is the parent of B' with respect to the covering relation, then either both are degenerate and connected by a blue seam edge or they have a vertex in common or there exists a spanning face F such that (ii) holds for F, B, and B'.*

Proof. (i) The seam leaves the face F as often as it enters it: thus the first and last vertices where it meets F either (a) coincide or (b) form the bounds on a chain of one or more green edges around F In the latter case, by definition, all edges in the chain belong to the same bridge B This proves the existence either of the unique spanning vertex in the case (a) or the spanning bridge B in case (b) (ii) Now let B' be any other bridge incident to F in a chain C of green edges, say (or possibly at a single seam vertex) The seam and the chain of edges meeting B (or v in the first case) between them surround a formation of one or more green components Each green component in this formation is simply connected, therefore C separates B' from the rest of this formation, and hence the seam cannot meet B' outside the span of the vertices bounding C (cf the argument illustrated in Figure 14) This implies that these are the extreme seam vertices on B', and the leftmost vertex in C is the root of the bridge B' under the conventions previously established Thus B covers B' Moreover, if B' covers some other bridge B'' it is clear that B'' is on the other side of the chain C so B'' cannot be incident to the face F (iii) If B and B' are on the same island (or mainland) or peninsula, there cannot be any chain of green edges separating these two bridges — otherwise B would not be the parent of B' it follows easily that there exists a green face to which both bridges are incident and (iii) holds in this case If B and B' are separated along the seam by at least one blue seam edge, then because of the existence of degenerate trees we are assured that they are incident to opposite ends of a unique seam edge The last case then is where B' is on a peninsula within the span of B but not containing B Again because of the existence of degenerate trees we know that the peninsula containing B' must have a point in common with the green component containing B at a point x, say, and it follows that either x is on B or x is separated from B by a spanning face which meets the seam within the span of B Q E D

Now the parent relation within the bridges themselves can be augmented to reflect the covering relation among the bridges, as follows Suppose that the vertex v or bridge B has been defined as in Lemma 25 (ii), if it is a bridge B rather than a single vertex which is in question, let v be the rightmost seam vertex on the spanning face meeting B Thus in either case we have distinguished a certain vertex v Then imagine the other incident bridges B' and multiple seam vertices v' in anticlockwise sequence about the face, connect the roots of these other bridges to v by adding fictitious (green) edges to the lobe, and make v the parent of all these roots In the case where v has several connectors incident to it, so it represents the leaf of more than one tree, ties may be broken arbitrarily, so long as only one of the leaves corresponding to v is chosen to be parent and the other leaves corresponding to v continue as leaves in the larger structure See figure 19 Similarly, the blue seam edges can be incorporated into the structure by regarding they themselves as forming links in the tree

The following lemma is then easily proved

Lemma 26 *With the addition of these fictitious edges and parent links, the set of green vertices and edges together with the seam vertices suitably replicated on the lobe acquires the structure of a single tree, whose root is the topmost vertex on the lobe*

Sketch of proof If F is any green face, then whether or not it is a spanning face we know that all bridges meeting the face are connected together (possibly through fictitious green edges) This implies that all vertices on the same green component are connected together The construction ensures also that vertices in different components are connected together by chains of parent links Since the topmost vertex on the lobe is a seam vertex and by definition it covers all other seam vertices, it becomes the root of the resulting binary structure Q E D

We are almost ready to build a balanced decomposition of a lobe The last requirement is to embed the structure in that of a binary tree This is quite standard if a node has $k \geq 3$ children, replace it by $k - 1$ fictitious nodes, form a complete binary tree with these as internal nodes and what were its children as leaves, and let the root of this new tree correspond to the original node The order of leaves in the new tree matches the order of the children of the original node Let T denote the resulting binary tree structure We shall call the tree T the *binary structure* of the lobe for which it was defined Using the tree decomposition technique as described in Section 4, we can find a vertex v in T such that the subtree T_v has between 1/3 and 2/3 as many nodes as T Let T'_v be the tree T with all proper descendants of T_v removed, and recursively

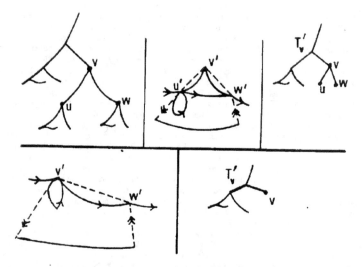

Figure 20: Illustrating cases (a) and (c) in Lemma 27.

decompose T_v and T_v''. This can be used to produce a balanced decomposition of the node by recursive near-splits, basing the method on the following

Lemma 27 *Let T be the binary structure of a lobe Λ. If T is decomposed as above into T_v and T_v', there exists a 1-, 2-, or 3-vertex near split of Λ into polytopes A and B such that T_v is the binary structure of A and T_v' that of B.*

Sketch of proof. The nodes of T correspond in a many-one fashion to the green vertices and connectors on the lobe. If x is a node of T let x' be the corresponding vertex or connector on the lobe. Given the node v, let u and w be the first vertices encountered in following the leftmost (respectively, rightmost) path down from v such that the corresponding entity u' (respectively, w') represents a seam vertex (more exactly, a connector). It is easy to see that in the chain $P = w'v'u'$ each pair of successive vertices is in the same green face (they need not be distinct). Furthermore it is easy to see that there is an interval $[i \ldots j]$ such that the seam vertices indexed in this interval consists precisely of those vertices x' such that x is a descendant of v in T. Therefore by Lemma 24 there is a Jordan curve J which surrounds precisely those vertices (and has at most 5 corners). Suppose that B represents that part within J and A that outside J in a near-split. Clearly T_v is the binary structure of B. The structure of A is almost as simple: it depends on how many of u', v', w' are distinct. (a) If they are all distinct we have a 3-vertex near split, and $u'v'w'$ defines a triangular green face above the seam; then T_v' almost reflects this structure: v should be given two children to represent the new connectors in A. (b) If they all coincide then the Jordan curve defines a triangular blue face in A and T_v' clearly reflects the structure of A. (c) If two of them coincide (necessarily $u' = v'$) then the curve defines two new blue faces, v represents a leaf vertex in the new structure and again T_v' represents the binary structure of A. See Figure 20. Q.E.D.

This decomposition proceeds until one arrives at a lobe with a bounded number of green faces. Then a line-query can be completed in logarithmic time because of the following

Lemma 28 *Let Λ be a lobe of a seam polytope with a bounded number of green faces, and suppose that a line-query has been localized to this lobe. Then with suitable preprocessing, the query can be completed in logarithmic serial time*

Proof Let us consider the case where the polytope has no green faces the more general case can be covered with some more attention to detail. In this case the polytope has a base, some back faces, and some blue faces, and all the blue faces meet the base the seam edges and vertices now form a treelike structure of blue edges. But this treelike structure is subject directly to Goodrich's decomposition technique and thus the polytope may be further decomposed by the methods already introduced. This ultimately reduces the query to a polytope with a bounded number of faces for which the query can be solved in $O(1)$ serial time Q E D

7.5 Computing the binary structure on a lobe.

In Subsection 7 4 we saw that each lobe carried a natural binary structure which could be exploited to enable efficient solution of line-queries against the lobe. It is not immediately clear how to compute this binary structure. Once the interconnection pattern among bridges has been established using fictitious green edges, to embed the structure in a binary tree is straightforward so we concentrate on identifying the bridges and forming the fictitious links.

To identify the bridges is straightforward once an eulerian circuit has been constructed to traverse each bridge (considered as a free tree), and, moreover, to construct such a circuit can easily be accomplished in $O(\log(n))$ parallel CREW time by assigning, say, one processor to each green vertex and one to each green edge incident to the vertex. Once this has been done, all edges in the same bridge can be identified in logarithmic parallel time using a pointer doubling method. Thus we can assume that each edge is given a label identifying the unique bridge containing it. Once this information is available, it is possible to identify the correct root vertex on each bridge. Next assigning one processor to each corner of each green face, it is possible to count the total number of seam vertices incident to each face. by comparing this to the range $[i \quad j]$ representing where the seam first and last meets the face, one can determine whether the face is a spanning face. Given a spanning face F it is possible (assigning one processor to each connector edge meeting the face) to identify those bridges incident to the face, and also those 'degenerate bridges' introduced above Lemma 25 can be identified with one processor per seam vertex meeting the face. All but at most one of these incident bridges will have their root vertex on the face, and this information tells us which vertex on the face is to be made the parent of the root vertices meeting the face using fictitious green edges. The order of incidence of these root vertices in anticlockwise order around the face can be ascertained in logarithmic parallel time using 'parallel prefix,' i.e, computing a cumulative sum of numbers around the face. In this way the interconnections among bridges can be established (to form links along blue seam edge, which the seam meets in both directions, is a straightforward variant problem). It is not difficult to splice the eulerian circuits for each bridge together with these new linkages to obtain an eulerian circuit for the whole interconnection structure. Finally the correct parent relation for this structure is easily computed using a trick of Tarjan and Vishkin's (1985) break the eulerian circuit at the root vertex, then use pointer jumping to compute the ranks of all entries in the resulting linked list. Then each edge is visited twice and it is visited first in the direction from parent to child. We therefore conclude the following

Lemma 29 *Given a lobe of a seam polytope, with the correct incidence relations established among its edges, faces, and vertices, and with the correct anticlockwise orderings of edges around faces and vertices, it is possible to compute in logarithmic parallel CREW time the binary structure of the lobe*

39

7.6 Building the seam polytope.

Much the same data-structures as have been employed in the previous discussion will serve to allow a recursive computation of the seam polytope Π It clarifies things slightly if we imagine the polytope to be split in two by a plane, so that the seam is no longer a closed circuit each part can be built separately and they can be combined at the end In the following lemma, the *true seam* of the polytope is that part of the seam which surrounds the mainland

Lemma 30 *Once the seam of the polytope has been found, the true seam can be identified, and the polytope can be split into two parts using a Jordan curve which divides the mainland transversally This Jordan curve is defined by a chain of four vertices connecting points on the seam by a path along the base, together with a plane whose intersection with the top and the mainland completes the circuit*

Proof Once the seam has been computed (and the base) it is straightforward to construct the true seam and sort it in logarithmic time using a running-sum technique We can therefore assume that the polytope has only one green component Also a suitable plane supporting the top can easily be found, and one green edge can be identified on the mainland, namely, that connecting the topmost seam vertex p to the top Let C be a plane through this edge cutting the polytope transversally at the edge Assigning one processor to each seam edge one can identify in logarithmic parallel time the point q closest to the top where a seam edge meets this plane on the other side of the top Choose seam vertices x and y sharing a blue face with p and q respectively Then the plane C and the chain $pxyq$ define a suitable Jordan curve Q E D

We can use this Jordan curve (formally) to split the polytope into two overlapping sub-polytopes A and B These polytopes have some new back faces' which are not relevant to the queries necessary for this section, it is not necessary to know all points along the Jordan curve described in Lemma 30 (This could be done in $O(\log^2(n))$ parallel time using a suboptimal planar convex hull algorithm Since we wish to construct the seam polytope using these structures recursively, this would not be appropriate) Splitting the polytope has little importance except that it means that the 'join' as defined below is a single zig-zag line like the 'contour' occurring in the construction of Voronoi diagrams in Section 4 First we assume that the green part of the polytope is connected, so the mainland is the only green component We use divide-and conquer choose a green seam edge e which is midway in rank along the seam Let X be the set of green and blue faces meeting the seam to the left of this point and Y the set meeting it to the right, recursively compute the polytopes defined by the top, base, back, and X (respectively, Y), and then compute their intersection Let us call the intermediate polytopes in this construction *partial seam-polytopes* These polytopes are essentially seam polytopes except they may be unbounded in one direction

Let the *join* denote the intersection of the 'mainlands' of two partial seam-polytopes Clearly the join meets the seam in a single green edge so it forms a zigzag chain of green edges and plays the role that the contour played in the context of the 2-dimensional Voronoi diagram Indeed the constructions are now so similar that it is enough to indicate some points about the present one

Definition 31 *A pure line-query is as follows given a semi-infinite ray R known to originate at a point interior to the core of a partial seam-polytope G, and not to be contained within G, to compute the point at which it leaves the polytope*

Lemma 32 *Assuming that the core and lobes are available for a partial seam-polytope G, with appropriate balanced decompositions any pure line-query can be solved in $O(\log(n))$ serial time Moreover, the exact coordinates of a solution vertex can be computed within the stated time*

Proof Let R be the ray given for a pure line-query Testing R for intersection with the top, base, or any blue face, or the back, can be done in logarithmic serial time by binary search If so, the query is solved Otherwise, another binary search will show where R leaves the core, this

40

solves the query or localizes it to a lobe Λ The localized query can be solved in logarithmic time as follows suppose $\Lambda = A \cup B$ is a near-split If R passes inside the Jordan curve bounding $A \cap B$ then the query is localized to the inner polytope, and moreover, the point where the given ray meets the back of the inner polytope can be computed in constant time Otherwise the query is localized to the outer polytope, thus the query is localized in constant time by testing R for intersection with $A \cap B$ Q E D

Given X and Y as mentioned above, let M and N be the associated partial seam-polytopes with the appropriate structures computed recursively Given a vertex v of X, one can find whether v is a vertex of the intersection as follows let p be some point interior to the base of $M \cap N$ p is easily computed, and serves as origin for a family of rays for pure line-queries

For any green vertex v of M, say, v is a vertex of $M \cap N$ if and only if the ray from p through v intersects the boundary of N beyond v Since the point where the ray meets the boundary can be computed exactly in $O(\log(n))$ time using the appropriate balanced decompositions, we can determine efficiently whether or not v belongs to the intersection

Thus the vertices of M may be retained or discarded as appropriate Similarly for the vertices of N An edge of M meets the join if and only if one end v is in the intersection and the other end w is not, the point where it meets the join can then be computed by solving a pure line-query for the ray beginning at v and passing through w The remainder of the 'merge' construction is very similar to that already described for the Voronoi diagram and we omit the details

This covers how to construct the seam polytope under the assumption that there are no green components except the mainland Notice that such components are ascertainable from the structure of the seam without constructing the seam polytope, as is the true seam, and it follows that a superset of the seam polytope (that obtained by deleting those green faces not on the mainland) can be constructed in $O(\log^2(n))$ parallel time This polytope possesses all the blue faces which the final seam polytope will possess

So far we have seen how to compute the seam polytope corresponding to the true seam It remains to account for the presence of other green components To do this we would proceed as follows For every green component separate from the mainland, one can find its topmost vertex v and two base vertices u and w which are adjacent to v (i e , which share a face with v) and such that the Jordan curve vuw surrounds all those green components within the span of v Thus using near-splits judiciously one can produce a formation of lobes, each of which possesses just one green component Within each lobe the green component can be built using the methods outlined above for constructing the mainland (Again it is convenient to split each structure into two sections using the method described in Lemma 30 It is not difficult to achieve this using the same methods as given in the Lemma) Since this fragmentation of parts of the seam polytope increases the total number of vertices in all the lobes by at most a linear factor, the construction can be accomplished in the same parallel time with n processors overall

Thus we have an $O(\log^2(n))$ $CREW$ construction of the seam polytope which leads to the $O(\log^3(n))$ construction of the convex hull, as asserted

7.7 A simpler approach.

This concludes our discussion of the convex hull problem The construction given here, while elaborate, matches the time-bounds of Anita Chow's, and does not require an optimal parallel sorting algorithm (Recall that the convex hull algorithm in [Chow (1980)] takes $O(\log^3(n) \log\log(n))$ parallel time, but the factor of $\log\log(n)$ arises from sorting and it can be removed by invoking optimal parallel sorting algorithms) We used information about the seams involved in the recursive construction to provide a search-structure to answer line-queries, and we introduced 'near-splitting' as a means to localize queries on our seam polytopes The method of near-splitting applies to any polytope whose corners can be evenly partitioned by a short polygonal Jordan curve around its boundary

The algorithm presented in the FOCS paper, worse by a factor of $\log(n)$, depended on adapting a variant of Kirkpatrick's planar decomposition method to a restricted kind of planar graph

Richard Cole (private communication) has suggested a simple method to apply Kirkpatrick's decomposition to *any* planar graph in parallel Let us say only that the decomposition was based on the observation that every planar graph has a substantial fraction of low-degree vertices (vertices of degree $k \leq 11$, say at least half the vertices have low degree in this sense) To develop a suitable search-structure, compute a maximal independent set of low-degree vertices, discard them, then triangulate and recursively reprocess the resulting planar graph For our application the 'planar graph' in question would be dual to a given convex polyhedron K (see [Dobkin and Kirkpatrick (1983)]) Richard Cole's suggestion is as follows to compute a maximal independent set of low-degree vertices, let G' be the graph formed by the edges incident to the low-degree vertices Construct a spanning forest of G', and let S be the subset of odd-depth vertices in this spanning forest (relative to an arbitrary assignment of roots for the trees in this forest) Since the trees have bounded degree, the size of S is a fixed fraction of the size of G' Let G'' be the subgraph of G' (or equivalently G) spanned by S, then every vertex in G'' has degree at most $k - 2$ (i e , 9) Repeating this process at most five more times we obtain a maximal independent set This method can be implemented to solve the convex hull problem with n processors in parallel time $\log^2(n)\alpha(n)$ where $\alpha(n)$ is the cost of constructing a spanning forest for instance, Shiloach and Vishkin's (1982) CRCW algorithm may be used in which case $\alpha(n)$ = $\log(n)$, thereby yielding a much simpler $NC_3^+(n)$ algorithm for the 3-D convex hull problem, though on a somewhat more powerful model of parallelism (concurrent write, the policy by which concurrent writes are resolved is immaterial to Shiloach and Vishkin's algorithm)

Recently Dadoun and Kirkpatrick (1987) showed that a Kirkpatrick decomposition could be built in $O(\log(n)\log^*(n))$ CREW time, thereby constructing the convex hull with an elegant $O(\log^2(n)\log^*(n))$ CREW algorithm

8 Final Remarks.

Although parallel algorithms in areas such as graph-theoretic algorithms and numerical problems, have been well-studied for several years already, a similar development is only beginning in computational geometry Consequently, even the most basic problems such as triangulation problems and those in geometric optimization have not been put in the class NC until this paper Standard techniques in the subject such as contour-tracing, plane-sweeping and gift-wrapping initially seem inherently sequential, one of our main contribution is to show that NC-analogues of these techniques actually exist As hinted before, efficient solutions to the basic problems imply correspondingly efficient solutions to a multitude of other problems, and we have only shown some of the reductions.

It is interesting to note that in the sequential setting, the problems of planar convex hulls, planar Voronoi diagrams, and 3-dimensional convex hulls all have the same $\Theta(n \log n)$ time complexity In the parallel case, these problems have been shown to be in

$$NC_1^*(n), NC_2^*(n), NC_3^*(n)$$

respectively Our planar convex hull algorithm, culminating several previous works, turns out to be optimal in a very strong sense and it remains open whether the parallel solutions for the other problems can be further improved.

Although all common problems in computational geometry are in NC [Kozen and Yap (1985)], we think that a main goal of parallel studies in computational geometry is to bring problems into the practical subclasses of NC In this paper we focused of $NC_k^*(n)$ for small k It is our belief that such algorithms (as opposed to $NC_k^*(n^2)$, say) will have practical implications In particular, it is possible that they could be employed in VLSI and in graphics machines or robots

ACKNOWLEDGEMENTS

Several people, including Richard Cole, David Kirkpatrick, Mi Lu, and Ivan Stojmenovic, noticed a false assumption in our Voronoi diagram algorithm in the original extended abstract. Ivan also provided an alternative merge procedure for of the Voronoi diagram algorithm Hubert Wagener pointed out the need for semi-edges in our Voronoi diagram algorithm Herbert Edelsbrunner pointed out that the seams could be non-simple in the 3-dimensional convex hull algorithm Finally, Prasoon Tiwari drew our attention to Anita Chow's valuable Ph D dissertation of 1980, which anticipated some of our results for the 3-dimensional convex hull her algorithm was actually better than the one presented at the 1985 FOCS conference

REFERENCES

A Aggarwal, J S Chang and C K Yap (1985)

'Minimum area circumscribing polygons ' *The Visual Computer* Vol 1 pp 112-117

A Aggarwal, M Klawe, S Moran, P Shor and R Wilber (1^86)

'Geometric applications of a matrix searching algorithm ' *Proc 2nd ACM Symposium on Computational Geometry* pp 285-292

M Ajtai, J Komlós, and E Szemerédi (1982)

'An O(n log (n)) Sorting Network ' *Proc 15th ACM Symposium on Theory of Computing,* pp 1-9 Also *Combinatorica* 3·1 *(1983)* pp 1-19

S Akl (1983)

'Parallel Algorithm for Convex Hulls' *manuscript*, Dept. of Comp Science, Queen's University, Kingston, Ontario

M.J Atallah, and M T Goodrich (1985)

'Efficient parallel solutions to geometric problems' *Proc 1985 IEEE Conf on Parallel Processing*, pp.411-417

M.J. Atallah, and M T. Goodrich (1986)

'Efficient plane sweeping in parallel' *Proc 2nd Symp on Computational Geometry*, pp 216-225

M.J Atallah, R Cole, and M T Goodrich (1987)

'Cascading divide-and-conquer a technique for designing parallel algorithms' To appear, *Proceedings 28th IEEE FOCS Symposium*

J L Bentley (1977)

'Algorithms for Klee's rectangle problems' *unpublished manuscript*, CMU

J L Bentley and D Wood (1980)

'An optimal worst case algorithm for reporting intersections of rectangles' *IEEE Trans on Comput* C-29 pp 571-577

M. Ben-Or (1983)

'Lower bounds for algebraic computationa trees' *15th STOC*, 80-86

M Ben-Or, D Kozen and J Reif (1984).

'The complexity of elementary algebra and geometry' *16th STOC*, pp 457-464

J E Boyce, D P Dobkin, R L Drysdale, L J Guibas (1985)

'Finding extremal polygons' *SIAM J Computing* 14 pp 134-147

R.P Brent (1974)

'The parallel evaluation of general arithmetic expressions' *J.ACM* 21.2 pp. 201-206

K Q Brown (1979)

'Voronoi diagrams from convex hulls' *Information Processing Letters*, 9.5, pp. 223-228

J S Chang (1986)

'Polygon Optimization Problems' *Ph.D Dissertation* Department of Computer Science, New York University Courant Robotics Report No 78, August 1986

B Chazelle (1982)

'A theorem on polygon cutting with applications' *Proc 23rd Symp on Found of Comput Sci*, pp 339-349

B M Chazelle (1984)

'Computational Geometry on a Systolic Chip' *IEEE Trans on Comp* C-33 pp 774-785

B Chazelle, J Incerpi (1984)

'Triangulation and Shape-Complexity' *ACM Trans on Graphics, Special Issue on "Computational Geometry*' 3:2, pp 135-152.

B Chazelle (1986)

'Reporting and Counting Segment Intersections' *Journal of Computer and System Sciences*, 32:2, pp 156-182

A Chow (1980)

'Parallel algorithms for geometric problems' Ph D Dissertation, Computer Science Department, University of Illinois at Urbana-Champaign, 1980.

A Chow (1981)

'A Parallel Algorithm for Determining Convex Hulls of Sets of Points in Two Dimensions' Proc 19th Allerton Conf on Comm Control and Computing, pp 214-233

V Chvátal (1975).

'A combinatorial theorem in plane geometry' Journal of Combinatorial Theory B, 18 pp 39-41

R Cole (1986)

'Parallel merge sort.' Proceedings 27th IEEE FOCS Symposium Toronto, Ontario, 511-516

R Cole and C Ó'Dúnlaing (1986)

'Note on the AKS sorting network' Technical Report #243 (Ultra #U109) Computer Science Department, New York University, September

G E Collins (1975)

'Quantifier elimination for real closed fields by cylindrical algebraic decomposition' 2nd GI Conference on Automata Theory and Formal Languages, Lecture Notes in Computer Science 33 (Springer-Verlag), pp 134-183

S Cook and C Dwork (1982)

'Bounds on the Time for Parallel RAMs to Compute Simple Functions' Proc 14th ACM Symposium on Theory of Computing, pp 231-233.

N Dadoun and D G Kirkpatrick (1987)

'Parallel processing for efficient subdivision search' Proceedings 3rd annual Symposium on Computational Geometry, Waterloo, Ontario, 1987, 205-214

D P Dobkin and D G Kirkpatrick (1983)

'Fast detection of polyhedral intersections' Theoretical Computer Science, 27 pp 241-253

H Freeman and R Shapira (1975)

'Determining the minimum-area encasing rectangle for an arbitrary closed curve' Communications ACM 18 7 (1975) 409-413

L J Guibas and J Stolfi (1983)

'Primitives for the manipulation of general subdivisions and the computation of Voronoi diagrams' Proceedings of the 15th ACM Symposium on Theory of Computing, pp 221-234 Also, to appear, ACM Transactions on Graphics

V Klee and M. C Laskowski (1985)

'Finding the smallest triangles containing a given polygon' J Algorithms, 6 pp 457-464

D Kozen and C K Yap (1985)

'Algebraic cell decomposition in NC' 26th FOCS, pp 515-521

T Leighton (1984)

Tight bounds on the complexity of parallel sorting Proceedings of the 16th ACM Symposium on Theory of Computing, pp 71-80

W Lipski Jr and F P Preparata (1981)

'Segments, rectangles, contours ' *J of Algorithms* 2, pp 63-76

D Nath, S N Maheshwari and P C P Bhatt (1981)

'Parallel Algorithms for the Convex Hull in Two Dimensions ' *Conference on Analysis Problem Classes and Programming for Parallel Computing*, pp 358-372

J O'Rourke, A Aggarwal, S Madilla and M Baldwin (1985)

'An optimal algorithm for finding minimal enclosing triangles ' *J Algorithms*, 7 2 (1986) 258-269

M H Overmars and J Van Leeuwen (1981)

'Maintenance of Configurations in the Plane.' *J of Computer and Systems Sciences*, 23, pp 166-204

F Preparata and S J Hong (1977)

'Convex hulls of finite sets of points in two and three dimensions ' *Communications of the ACM* 20 pp 87-93

F Preparata and M I Shamos (1985)

'Computational Geometry an Introduction ' Springer, 1985

M I Shamos (1977)

'Computational geometry ' Ph D dissertation, Yale University.

M I Shamos and D Hoey (1975)

'Closest point problems ' *Proceedings of the 16th IEEE Symposium on Foundations of Computing*, pp 151-162

Y Shiloach and U Vishkin (1982)

'An $O(\log(n))$ parallel connectivity algorithm ' *J Algorithms* 3 (1982) 57-67

R.E. Tarjan and U Vishkin, (1985)

'An efficient parallel biconnectivity algorithm ' *SIAM J on Comput* , 14.4, pp 862-874

G. T Toussaint (1983)

'Solving geometric problems using 'rotating callipers ' *Proceedings IEEE Melecon '83* Athens, Greece

H Wagener (1985)

'Parallel Computational Geometry Using Polygon Ordering ' Ph D Thesis, Technical University of Berlin, FRG (1985)

H Wagener (1987)

'Optimally parallel algorithms for convex hull determination ' Submitted for publication

L G Valiant (1975)

'Parallelism in comparison problems ' *SIAM Journal on Computing* 4.3 pp 348-355

C K Yap (1987)

'What can be parallelized in computational geometry?' *International Workshop on Parallel Algorithms and Architecture, Humboldt University, Berlin, DDR (Invited talk) Proceedings to appear in Springer-Verlag volume*